Financial Accounting

To Deena, Goshi, Raf, Shabbir, Shoaib
and the class of '82

SAGE COURSE COMPANIONS

KNOWLEDGE AND SKILLS *for* SUCCESS

Financial Accounting

John Stittle and
Robert Wearing

SAGE Publications
Los Angeles · London · New Delhi · Singapore

SAGE Publications Ltd
1 Oliver's Yard
55 City Road
London EC1Y 1SP

SAGE Publications Inc.
2455 Teller Road
Thousand Oaks, California 91320

SAGE Publications India Pvt Ltd
B 1/I 1 Mohan Cooperative Industrial Area
Mathura Road
New Delhi 110 044

SAGE Publications Asia-Pacific Pte Ltd
33 Pekin Street #02-01
Far East Square
Singapore 048763

Library of Congress Control Number available

British Library Cataloguing in Publication data

A catalogue record for this book is available from the British Library

ISBN 978-1-4129-3502-9
ISBN 978-1-4129-3503-6 (pbk)

Typeset by C&M Digitals (P) Ltd., Chennai, India
Printed in India at Replika Press Pvt. Ltd
Printed on paper from sustainable resources

contents

This Sage Course Companion offers you an insider's guide into how to make the most of your financial accounting course, and extend your understanding of key concepts. It will provide you with essential help with revising for your course exams, preparing and writing course assessment materials, and enhancing and progressing your knowledge and thinking skills in line with course requirements.

It isn't intended to replace your textbooks or lectures – it is intended to save you time when you are revising for your exams or preparing coursework. Note that RE-vision implies that you looked at the subject the first time round!

The Companion will help you to anticipate exam questions, and gives guidelines on what your examiners will be looking for. It should be seen as a framework in which to organise the subject matter, and to extract the most important points from your textbooks, lecture notes, and other learning materials on your course.

This book is intended to direct you to the key issues in financial accounting. Whichever textbook you are using, the basics are the basics: we have given some guidance on where topics are covered in specific books, but you should read the Companion in parallel with your textbook and identify where subjects are covered in more detail in both your textbook and in your course syllabus.

How to use this book

This book should be used as a supplement to your textbook and lecture notes. You may want to glance through it quickly, reading it in parallel with your course syllabus, and note where each topic is covered in both the syllabus and this Companion. Ideally, you should buy this book at the beginning of your course – it will provide you with a quick explanation of any topics you are having trouble with. But if you buy the book towards the end of your course you should find it a valuable aid in your revision.

Part 2 introduces and explains the important elements of the core syllabus. Your lectures and textbook should give you a good grounding in the basics. However, financial accounting concepts are not always easy to master the first time round, so the more you read and practise typical exercises and questions, the more confident you will feel when you get to the examination.

The sections in Part 2 contain the following features:

- **Tips** to help you remember important points and understand how you can earn additional marks in the exam.
- **Numerical examples and questions** which you can work through and which will help to reinforce your understanding of basic concepts. Answers are provided to all worked examples and questions.
- **Textbook guides** where reference is made to appropriate chapters from financial accounting textbooks for additional reading.

There is also a guide to study, writing and revision skills in Part 3 which will help you to learn more efficiently. Learning is best accomplished by seeing the information from several different angles – which is why you attend lectures and tutorials, read the textbook, and read around the subject in general. This book will help you to bring together these different sources.

Finally, it is often remarked that financial accounting is ultimately a means of communicating information; in effect it is the language of business. Do not fall into the trap of thinking that, because something cannot be measured, it does not exist. Although much of financial accounting involves numbers, never forget that a considered and thoughtful approach will help you to appreciate the full significance of those numbers.

part two

core areas of the curriculum

1

introduction to financial accounting, stewardship and regulation

Accounting classifications

Accounting is frequently divided into two major categories:

1 Financial accounting, and

2 Management accounting.

Financial accounting is primarily concerned with recording, processing and presenting historic information for the benefit of users external to the business. This area of accounting is concerned with preparing accounts for a business and then interpreting the information. Financial accounting is subject to a detailed regulatory framework of accounting and legal rules.

Management accounting is aimed at providing information to enable managers to operate, control and plan the future direction of their business. Management accounting includes topics such as costing, budgeting and the planning of resources.

Management accounting is largely unregulated by accounting and legal frameworks.

In this book, we are only concerned with financial accounting.

Financial accounting

In your studies of financial accounting, you must understand how to collect and record data, prepare a **trial balance** and produce various types of business **financial statements**. In this book the most important financial statements are covered and these consist of the:

- trading and profit and loss account
- **balance sheet**
- cash flow statement.

You will also be required to understand the nature of accounting adjustments that businesses frequently have to make to financial data and, importantly, be able to interpret the final financial statements.

You must also understand why financial statements are prepared, their purpose and the types of organisations and individuals who are commonly interested in reading them.

Stewardship

Traditionally, ensuring high standards of 'stewardship' has been seen as an important objective of financial accounting. In many businesses, managers and directors are trusted with taking care of business assets on behalf of the legal owners. For example, shareholders are the legal owners of a company's assets but the directors of a **company** control and manage the **assets** on a day-to-day basis on behalf of, or in trust for the shareholders. In other words, the directors are said to have 'stewardship' of the company's assets.

In the UK, the largest companies are referred to as quoted or listed companies, that is they are quoted or listed on the London Stock Exchange. Such companies can be identified by the letters **Plc** (public limited company) after their name. One of these large companies might have several billion shares and several hundred thousand shareholders. These shareholdings are often fragmented, which means that no single individual on their own is in a position to control the operations of the company. Even large pension funds and insurance companies own only a small proportion of the total shares. In these circumstances, it is often said that in modern large quoted companies there is a separation of ownership and control. Separation of ownership and control means that the shareholders (owners) are separate from the board of directors who control the company. It is therefore vital that the owners receive good quality information (via the financial statements) so that they can judge how well (or, perhaps, how badly!) the company's affairs are being managed. The auditors also have a major role to play in ensuring that the financial statements which have been prepared by the company's accountants, give a **true and fair view** of its financial performance and financial position at the accounting year end.

Accountability

Stewardship is usually linked with the term **accountability**. In a business, 'accountability' means explaining your actions and decisions. For example, the directors of a company will have to be accountable to the **shareholders** because they are looking after (i.e. have 'stewardship') of the company's assets. At the end of the financial year, the directors will explain what they have achieved with the shareholders' assets – such as the level of **profits** they have obtained by using the assets. The directors' explanation is conventionally communicated to shareholders through the preparation of the annual report and accounts.

Over the years the annual report and accounts have become more and more complex. It is now not uncommon for the annual report and accounts of a large company to run to 200 pages. Nevertheless, the fundamental principles of accounting apply, whether we are considering the largest quoted company or the smallest private limited company (those which have the letters **Ltd** after their name, denoting private limited company and whose shares are not traded on a **stock** exchange).

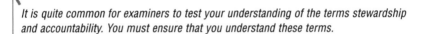

It is quite common for examiners to test your understanding of the terms stewardship and accountability. You must ensure that you understand these terms.

Regulation

Over the years, government and regulatory bodies have become increasingly interested in monitoring and regulating the quality and quantity of information provided by companies to their investors and other users. The main regulations which **limited liability** companies have to observe are those based on *company law* and also *accounting standards*.

Company law

In the UK, companies with limited liability must conform to the provisions of the **Companies Acts** which have been enacted by Parliament. For instance, the requirement to carry out an **audit** is imposed by company law and if you look at the auditor's report for any large company it will usually include a statement to the effect that the financial statements have been properly prepared in accordance with the Companies Act 1985 and that they give a 'true and fair view' of the state of the company's affairs at the year end and of its profit and **cash flows** for the financial year.

Accounting standards

Companies are also required to comply with accounting standards. These can take the form of UK accounting standards or international accounting standards.

In the UK, private limited companies are required to comply with accounting standards issued by the **Accounting Standards Board (ASB)**. The ASB is itself supervised by the **Financial Reporting Council (FRC)**. In the UK, accounting standards are technically referred to as **financial reporting standards (FRS)** and these have been produced by the ASB since 1991 when the very first FRS (FRS 1, *Cash Flow Statements*) was published. Before 1991 the predecessor body of the ASB was the Accounting Standards Committee (ASC) which published **Statements of Standard Accounting Practice (SSAP)**. Some of those SSAPs are still valid today, so that UK accounting standards now consist of a mixture of SSAPs and FRSs.

International accounting standards

Until 2005 it was also the case that quoted companies in the UK were required to comply with UK accounting standards. But it is important to be aware that the UK is becoming increasingly influenced by the changes which are taking place in international accounting standards. The growth in **international accounting standards** has largely been encouraged by stock markets around the world who want one consistent set of accounting standards to apply to all companies. A main reason is that companies based in different countries are often keen to be listed on international stock exchanges.

The terminology used in this context is sometimes confusing so let's try to clarify what is going on. The idea of accounting standards, which could be used internationally, goes back over 30 years when the **International Accounting Standards Committee (IASC)** was formed. Then in the 1990s, as investors were becoming attracted to the idea of investing in companies in foreign countries, the notion of international standards found substantial support. The old IASC was substantially reorganised and renamed as the **International Accounting Standards Board (IASB)**. In order to distinguish new standards from the old standards, the new standards were given a different title: **International financial reporting standards (IFRS)**. So the current set of international standards includes both IAS and IFRS. The problem is that when you read the financial press, discussion often uses terms such as 'international standards', 'international accounting standards' or 'international financial reporting standards' to mean more or less the same thing. But usually you can tell by the context of an article what is intended.

Another factor promoting the importance of international accounting standards is the fact that the European Union has required quoted companies (from 2005 onwards) to comply with international standards (that is IAS and IFRS). To be precise, the European Union (EU) requires all quoted companies in the EU to comply with international accounting standards for accounting years beginning 1 January 2005 or thereafter. Non-quoted companies (that is, companies which do not have a stock exchange quotation) in the UK may implement international accounting standards, if they wish, but there is not yet a requirement to do so. It is likely that most UK non-quoted companies will not use international accounting standards for some years yet.

For the purposes of this book we intend to concentrate on the *principles* of accounting rather than the detailed *rules*. It is fortunate that UK accounting standards are broadly similar in many respects to international accounting standards. There are some differences though. For instance, international accounting standards refer to the **income statement** whereas UK accounting standards refer to the **profit and loss account**. International accounting standards refer to 'receivables' whereas UK accounting standards refer to **debtors**. Since the UK is in a period of transition as it learns to adjust to the new international accounting standards, we will be incorporating both types of terminology.

Types of businesses

There are a number of types of businesses that are required to produce accounts:

1. **Sole trader** – this is where an individual is also the owner of the business.

2. **Partnership** – this is where at least two individuals decide to operate a business – usually sharing profits and losses.

3. Limited company (larger companies may be termed public limited companies) – this is where the limited company is treated as a separate legal entity from its owners (shareholders).

4 Other organisations such as central and local government, social clubs, voluntary organisations and charities. These types of organisations often place more emphasis on providing a service for the public (or for the organisation's members) rather than primarily concentrating on making a profit.

User groups

When you are preparing accounts, it is useful to remember just whom you are preparing the information for and for what purposes users might require the information.

Key user groups

The key users of financial accounting information are usually identified as:

- shareholders/investors;
- trade **creditors** and suppliers;
- employees;
- banks and other financial institutions;
- customers;
- others – such as the government, financial analysts and the public.

- Shareholders (both actual and potential investors) may find information in the financial statements to assist in evaluating the profitability of their actual or proposed investment in the organisation. These users may wish to attempt to assess future growth potential and perhaps evaluate whether a company will have, for example, the resources to pay a **dividend.**
- Trade creditors and suppliers may use the financial statements to attempt to assess whether it appears that an organisation is credit worthy and will be able to pay for the goods that have been supplied on **credit**.
- Employees and trade unions may be interested in financial statements to attempt to assess whether the organisation appears to be in a position to continue trading in the future (known as being a **going concern**). This going concern concept is important in helping employees to assess whether they will have future continuity of employment. Trade unions and employees might also wish to use accounting information in salary and wage negotiations to assess whether an organisation has the resources to deliver a higher pay offer.
- Banks and other financial institutions may wish to use accounting information to assess whether an organisation should be granted a loan. In particular, banks will want to ensure that an organisation appears to have assets that can be used as collateral or security for a loan or mortgage. Banks will also

wish to assess whether organisations have, or will have, sufficient cash flow in order to meet the interest payments on loans.

- Customers who undertake business with an organisation might wish to judge whether an organisation can continue to trade and not cease operations in the near future – which might also cause disruption to their business as well.
- There are also other groups in society that are interested such as the public and other special interest groups. Many organisations such as multinational companies are large enough to be able to exercise economic and political influence in society. As a result, members of the public and pressure groups may wish to monitor their accounts in an attempt to find any information that can be used to make these organisations more accountable for their actions and policies. National and local government may find some reported information useful for national and local monitoring and planning purposes.

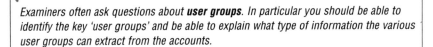

*Examiners often ask questions about **user groups**. In particular you should be able to identify the key 'user groups' and be able to explain what type of information the various user groups can extract from the accounts.*

Limitations of financial statements

However, there are a number of limitations of financial accounting information that affect all the above user groups. For example, the information in the accounts is often out of date and restricted in its use by the time it is published. Companies can take many months to produce their financial statements after their year end – which means that the information may have restricted or limited use because of its age. For potential shareholders in particular, it may be too late to decide to purchase shares by the time the financial statements have been prepared and released.

Likewise, banks and other lending institutions also find the accounts too limited in the information they require in assessing the eligibility of a business for a loan. Many banks will require more recent accounts and quite often will require information from the management accounts.

Modern finance theory also refers to the idea of efficient capital markets, whereby share prices rapidly move up and down to reflect new or unexpected information. One of the interesting implications of the **efficient markets hypothesis** (EMH) is that an individual investor, on their own, is not able to consistently achieve a superior investment return compared to the return achieved by the market. An exception might possibly be if an individual possessed superior analytical skills compared to other investors in the market.

Financial accounting has an important role to play in making sure that financial statements provide investors and others with the information they need to make their decisions and that this information is provided in a timely manner to relevant users.

Accounting policies

Companies need to produce their financial statements by adopting a number of accounting policies.

FRS 18, *Accounting Policies,* describes accounting policies as the 'principles, bases, conventions, rules and practices applied by an entity that specify how the effects of transactions and other events are to be reflected in the financial statements ...' (see FRS 18, para. 4). Companies should select those accounting policies 'judged to be the most appropriate to its particular circumstances for the purpose of giving a true and fair view' (see FRS 18, para. 17).

These policies typically explain how a company has treated such issues as fixed assets, research and development, foreign currency, stocks and pensions, etc.

FRS 18 makes a distinction between *accounting policies* and *estimation techniques.* For example, in relation to fixed assets, a firm's *accounting policy* might be to show these items at the cost of purchase less provisions for depreciation and impairment. The firm's choice of *estimation technique* for depreciation might be the reducing balance method (instead of, say, straight line method).

In addition there are four accounting concepts that play a particularly significant role in financial statements, namely, going concern, accruals, consistency and prudence.

Going concern concept

This concept requires companies to prepare their financial statements on the going concern basis, in other words, it is assumed that the business will continue in operational existence for the foreseeable future and has no intention to curtail operations significantly.

Accruals concept

Under this concept, (sometimes referred to as 'matching') it is assumed that companies use the **accruals concept** to prepare their financial statements. The accruals concept means that companies should prepare their financial statements by accounting for transactions as and when they arise or are incurred and not necessarily when any cash involved is received or paid.

Consistency concept

Under this concept, companies should adopt similar accounting treatments from one year to the next. In other words they should not change their accounting treatment in order to produce a favourable result in their accounts.

Prudence concept

Under this concept, revenues and profits are not anticipated, but are only recognised when realised in the form of cash or other assets (such as debtors). On the other hand, provision is made for expenses and losses even though they can only be estimated. This concept implies that firms are likely to err on the side of conservatism when preparing their accounts.

It is useful to note that international accounting standards and UK accounting standards regard going concern and accruals as the two most important concepts and FRS 18 argues that consistency and prudence are 'desirable qualities of information rather than the bedrock of accounting' (see FRS 18, App. IV, para. 12).

Realisation

FRS18 also highlights the importance of the term: realisation. In preparing financial statements, a company should 'have regard to requirements in companies legislation that only profits realised at the balance sheet date should be included in the profit and loss account ... profits shall be treated as realised ... only when realised in the form either of cash or of other assets the ultimate cash realisation of which can be assessed with reasonable certainty' (FRS 18, para. 28).

Objectives in selecting accounting policies

The objectives against which a company should judge the appropriateness of its accounting policies are:

Relevance

Financial information is relevant 'if it has the ability to influence the economic decisions of users ...' (see FRS 18, para. 33). A company should select those accounting policies that 'will result in financial information being presented that is relevant'. Information is regarded as being 'relevant' if it has the ability to influence the economic decisions of users and is provided in time to influence those decisions.

Reliability

Financial information is reliable if:

a   it can 'be depended upon by users to represent faithfully (what) ... it purports to represent and therefore reflects the substance of the transactions and other events that have taken place';
b   it is free from deliberate or systematic bias (i.e. it is neutral);
c   it is free from material error;
d   it is complete within the bounds of materiality;
e   under conditions of uncertainty, it has been prudently prepared (a degree of caution has been applied in exercising judgement and making the necessary estimates)
    (see FRS 18, para. 35).

Comparability

Appropriate accounting policies will result in financial information that is comparable over time and between companies in the same business sector. Comparability can usually be achieved through a combination of consistency and disclosure.

Understandability

Financial information must be readily understandable by users. It is assumed that the users of accounting information have a reasonable knowledge of business and economic activities and accounting and have a willingness to study this information with a reasonable degree of diligence. However, this description does not mean that complex material should be omitted or ignored. Complex financial information may be significant because it is relevant to assist users make economic decisions.

Overall, a company's accounting policies should be reviewed regularly to ensure they continue to provide a true and fair view.

> *Make sure that you understand and can explain these key terms: going concern, accruals, consistency, prudence, realisation, **relevance**, **reliability**, comparability and understandability.*

Information sources

Don't forget that there is a great deal of information available on the web – learn to take maximum advantage of this resource. For example the ASB and IASB have very informative websites which give historical background to the development of these organisations and progress on new accounting standards. For the ASB see www.asb.org.uk and for the IASB see www.iasb.org.uk. The large accounting firms also have informative websites and it is helpful to keep in touch with them. For instance Deloitte (www.deloitte.co.uk) publish *IFRS in Your Pocket*, a useful summary of current international accounting standards. This publication can be downloaded as a pdf from www.iasplus.com.

EXAMPLE QUESTION

What do you understand by the term 'user groups'? With reference to *two* user groups of your choice explain the nature and use of the information that these users could obtain from financial statements.

Suggested answer

A full answer to this question could usefully include the following points:

- User groups refer to those groups who might benefit from the financial information produced by an organisation.
- User groups may not necessarily have a legal commitment or contract with the firm but could include members of the public who might be interested in, say, environmental issues.
- Briefly compare and contrast different types of user such as shareholders, lenders, customers and suppliers.
- Choose two types of user and discuss their different information needs. It would be a good idea to choose users who have contrasting information needs and this will make an interesting answer. Your choice could be, say, shareholders and employees.
- Shareholders are interested in forward looking information and need information which will help them predict the firm's future profitability since this will have an impact on future dividends and share prices. Thus the profit and loss account will provide useful information on sales revenues, the profile of costs and also **earnings** per share.
- Information on asset values will help shareholders to contrast the book value of the assets of the company with the market value (or market **capitalisation**). A market capitalisation which is relatively high to the book value might indicate that the market has confidence in the firm's future growth prospects.
- Information on **equity** and gearing levels can help to indicate the level of risk associated with the firm.
- Employees are likely to be interested in the level of wage increases that the firm can afford as well as their future job security.
- As regards wage increases, employees (and their representatives, such as trade unions) will be interested in the level of profitability. Can the firm pay increased levels of wages and benefits without jeopardising future investment in productive assets?
- Is the firm financially sound? In other words can it continue or increase current levels of production without fear of liquidation of some or all of its divisions?
- Does the company's pension scheme show a deficit and, if so, what steps is management taking to try to reduce the deficit?

Textbook guide

ATRILL AND MCLANEY: *Chapter 1*
BRITTON AND WATERSTON: *Chapter 1*
HAND, ISAAKS AND SANDERSON: *Chapter 7*
JONES: *Chapters 1 and 2*

2

the accounting equation and recording transactions

Double entry **bookkeeping** is based on the idea that each business transaction has two effects. We can approach this idea by understanding that a business comprises a collection of assets. And for all those assets there are claims on the assets. At its most basic we can consider the **balance sheet** identity as follows:

Balance sheet identity

Assets   = Claims

economic resources expected   title to, or interests in the resources
to benefit future activities   of the entity

The balance sheet represents a picture of the business at a particular point in time. We can think of assets as economic resources which will benefit the business entity in the future. For instance, firms buy plant and machinery because they believe that these assets will generate revenues in the future which will be substantially greater than the costs of buying the original assets and operating them.

At the same time, someone (or some organisation) is entitled to the assets and net benefits which will be generated. This entitlement we can call 'claims'. These claims might be those of suppliers who have not yet been paid, employees whose wages have not yet been paid, banks who have lent money to the business and shareholders who have invested money in the business by purchasing shares. This is what we mean by the balance sheet identity, that is, the total assets of the business must be equal to all of the claims against those assets.

Next, we can expand the balance sheet identity and consider the **accounting equation**. In the accounting equation we separate the claims into those of the owners (which we call **equity**) and the remaining claims (which we call liabilities).

Accounting equation

Assets (A)	=	Liabilities (L)	+	Owners' equity (OE)
For example:		For example:		For example:
Cash		Banks		Shareholders
Stock		Suppliers		
Land		Employees		or
Building		Tax authorities		
Machinery				Proprietor (sole trader)

For simplicity we can refer to assets as 'A', liabilities as 'L' and owners' equity as 'OE'.

We can also take the equation:

$$A = L + OE$$

And rearrange it to give:

$$OE = A - L$$

Which simply says that the owners' equity consists of the firm's total assets less the total liabilities.

The category of owners' equity requires some additional explanation. In the case of a listed company (Plc) or private limited company (Ltd), the claim of the shareholders would be the amount of their original investment when they first subscribed for shares in the company. It would subsequently include their share of any profits generated by the company in later years.

Do not forget that sometimes companies generate losses and this is obviously bad news for shareholders! In these cases the losses will reduce the amount of owners' equity. In extreme cases the losses can wipe out the original investment of the shareholders which results in negative equity.

EXAMPLE

Sophie starts a business 'Sophie's Craft Shop' and on day one she:

(a) puts £5,000 of her own money into the business, and
(b) arranges a business loan of £4,000 from the bank.

We can now consider the effect of these initial transactions on the accounts of the business:

(a) represents an injection of capital by the owner (Sophie). She has written a cheque for £5,000 on her private bank account and paid the money into a newly created business bank account.

(b) involves the business borrowing £4,000 from the bank.

The above information gives a clue to the double entry accounting treatment, that is, the double sided nature of these transactions. We can represent this information in terms of the accounting equation as follows:

assets (A)	=	liabilities (L)	+	owners' equity (OE)
(a) £5,000 cash				£5,000 capital
(b) £4,000 cash		£4,000 bank loan		_____
£9,000		£4,000		£5,000

> Text books are not always very clear in distinguishing between 'cash' and 'bank'. In the above illustration, you can assume that the £9,000 cash (£5,000 + £4,000) is deposited in the business bank account. It is normally the case that 'cash' in these types of example means 'cash at bank and in hand'.

Well, the first day of business has not exactly been exciting. No trading took place. Nevertheless, it is possible to draw up a (very simple) balance sheet. In fact, in theory, a balance sheet can be drawn up at any time, although it is usual to draw them up at regular intervals such as the end of the month, end of three months or end of the financial year.

So here is the balance sheet:

Sophie's Craft Shop: balance sheet at the end of day one

Assets	£
Cash	9,000
Less Liabilities	
Bank loan	4,000
	5,000
Owner's equity	
Capital introduced	5,000

It is now time to expand our basic accounting equation and make the distinction between current assets (CA) and fixed assets (FA). Current assets are those assets which the business uses frequently in its day-to-day trading operations. These assets include cash, stock and debtors. Stock refers to those goods which the business buys in order to sell on to customers. Because customers do not always pay immediately for the goods they have received, the money they owe to the business is called **debtors** or 'accounts receivable'. Fixed assets are those assets which the business intends to keep for the long term, such as land, buildings, machinery and vehicles.

We can also differentiate between long term liabilities (LTL) and short term liabilities (STL). An example of a long term liability would be a bank loan which may be repaid some years into the future. A short term liability would be a supplier who requires payment for goods or services supplied after, say, one month. Short term liabilities are normally those repayable within one year. Long term liabilities are normally those repayable after one year.

Finally we can differentiate between the capital introduced by the owner (CI) and profits generated subsequently, or **retained profits** (RP). The total of these two figures represents owner's equity.

Our original accounting equation:

$$\text{assets (A)} = \text{liabilities (L)} + \text{owners' equity (OE)}$$

can now be restated as:

$$FA + CA = STL + LTL + CI + RP$$

Where:

```
FA  = fixed assets
CA  = current assets
STL = short term liabilities
LTL = long term liabilities
CI  = capital introduced
RP  = retained profits
```

On day two Sophie becomes more adventurous and:

(c) buys furniture and fittings for £2,500, payable in two months' time;

(d) pays £1,800 cash to buy goods for resale;

(e) sells half the goods to a customer for £1,300;

(f) withdraws £450 from the bank for her personal use.

In terms of the accounting equation, the effect of the above transactions is as follows:

FA	+	CA	=	STL	+	LTL	+	CI	+	RP
b/f		£9,000 cash				£4,000		£5,000		
(c) £2,500				£2,500						
(d)		−£1,800 cash								
(d)		£1,800 goods								
(e)		−£900 goods								−£900 cos
(e)		£1,300 debtor								£1,300 sale
(f)		−£450						−£450		
£2,500		£8,950		£2,500		£4,000		£4,550		£400

In transaction (c) above the increase in fixed assets of £2,500 has been 'balanced' by the increase in short term liabilities of the same amount.

Note that in transaction (d) above, there is no overall change to current assets, since cash has been reduced by £1,800, but goods (for resale) have been increased by £1,800.

It is important to understand the effect of transaction (e) on the business. Firstly, half the goods were sold to the customer. The result of this is to reduce stock by one half (from £1,800 to £900), that is, current assets are reduced by £900. Also, we have to remember the impact on owner's equity. We have to charge the business with the **cost of sales** (cos) of £900 and the effect of this is to reduce retained profit by £900.

Next we have to consider the value of the debtor which has been created. The value of the sale was £1,300, so current assets (debtors) increase by £1,300. In addition, the sales revenue of £1,300 represents an increase in retained profit to the business.

The final transaction (f) represents a reduction in cash of £450 and also a reduction in the capital of the business. Withdrawals of capital by an owner are often referred to as 'drawings'.

We can now draw up the balance sheet for Sophie's business at the end of day two.

Sophie's Craft Shop: balance sheet at the end of day two

	£	£
Assets		
Fixed assets		2,500
Cash		8,950
		11,450
Less **liabilities**		
Short term creditor	2,500	
Bank loan	4,000	6,500
		4,950
Owner's equity		
Capital introduced		5,000
Less: drawings		450
		4,550
Add: profit for period		400
		4,950

EXAMPLE QUESTIONS

Question 1

For each of the following transactions, you are required to show the effect on the assets, liabilities and owners' equity. Use + for increase, – for decrease and 0 for no change.

You are advised to use the following accounting equation format:

event	fixed assets	+	current assets	=	liabilities	+	owners' equity
1	+300,000		+200,000	=			+500,000

1 In the formation of a company, the owners contribute a building worth £300,000 and cash of £200,000.

2 Office equipment costing £12,000 is purchased. A deposit of £4,000 cash is made, with the balance due in 90 days.

3 A bank loan of £50,000 is taken out.

4 Goods costing £120,000 are purchased on credit.

5 £60,000 of goods are sold to a customer on credit. The goods originally cost the company £48,000.

6 Building improvements costing £37,000 are made. The amount is payable in three months' time.

Question 2

Fill in the missing amounts indicated by the variables x, y and z in the following table. Treat each case as an independent situation. Note that t_0 and t_1 refer to the opening balance sheet and closing balance sheet respectively.

	Case no. 1 £	Case no. 2 £	Case no. 3 £
Assets t_0	(x)	42,000	42,000
Assets t_1	70,500	42,000	(x)
Liabilities t_0	16,500	27,000	19,500
Liabilities t_1	13,500	(x)	12,000
Owners' equity t_0	30,000	(y)	(y)
Owners' equity t_1	(y)	16,000	27,500
Additional capital paid in	(z)	(z)	7,000
Revenues	106,000	48,000	(x)
Expenses	102,000	50,500	39,800

Solutions to questions

Question 1

Event	Fixed assets	+	Current assets	=	Liabilities	+	Owners' Equity
1	+300,000		+200,000	=			+500,000
2	+12,000		−4,000	=	+8,000		
3			+50,000	=	+50,000		
4			+120,000	=	+120,000		−
5			+60,000	=			+60,000
			−48,000	=			−48,000
6	+37,000			=			+37,000

> In a transaction which involves the sale of goods at a price higher *than the original cost,* you must remember to charge the cost of the goods to owners' equity (as an expense) and treat the revenue received as an addition to owner's equity.

Question 2

Case 1

$$\text{Assets } t_0 \quad = \quad \text{Liabilities } t_0 \quad + \quad \text{Owners' equity } t_0$$
$$x \quad = \quad 16,500 \quad + \quad 30,000$$

Therefore, assets t_0 = **46,500**

$$\text{assets } t_1 \quad = \quad \text{liabilities } t_1 \quad + \quad \text{owners' equity } t_1$$
$$70,500 \quad = \quad 13,500 \quad + \quad y$$

Therefore, owners' equity t_1 = **57,000**

owners' equity t_1	=	owners' equity t_0	+	additional capital	+	profit for period (R − P)
57,000	=	30,000	+	z	+	(106,000 − 102,000)
57,000	=	30,000	+	z	+	4,000

Therefore, additional capital paid in = **23,000**

Case 2

assets t_1		liabilities t_1		owners' equity t_1
42,000	=	x	+	16,000
	=		+	

Therefore, liabilities t_1 = **26,000**

assets t_0		liabilities t_0		owners' equity t_0
42,000	=	27,000	+	y
	=		+	

Therefore, owners' equity t_0 = **15,000**

owners' equity t_1		owners' equity t_0		additional capital		profit for period (R–P)
16,000	=	15,000	+	z	+	(48,000–50,500)
16,000	=	15,000	+	z	–	2,500

Therefore, additional capital paid in = **3,500**

Case 3

assets t_1		liabilities t_1		owners' equity t_1
x	=	12,000	+	27,500
	=		+	

Therefore, assets, t_1 = **39,500**

assets t_0		liabilities t_0		owners' equity t_0
42,000	=	19,500	+	y
	=		+	

Therefore, owners' equity, t_0 = **22,500**

owners' equity t_1		owners' equity t_0		additional capital		profit for period (R–P)
27,500	=	22,500	+	7,000	+	z – 39,800

Therefore, revenue = **37,800**

Textbook guide

ATRILL AND MCLANEY: *Chapter 2*
BRITTON AND WATERSTON: *Chapter 2*
JONES: *Chapter 3*

3
accruals and prepayments

Accruals and **prepayments** lie at the heart of the double entry **bookkeeping** system and modern financial accounting. The **accruals concept** is often used to refer to both accruals (outstanding or unpaid expenses) and prepayments (payments in advance). You may remember that earlier in this part we discussed some of the accounting concepts and, in particular, we stressed the importance of the accruals concept where the accruals concept refers to the process of *matching revenue and expenses* of the *same* accounting period.

A business will prepare its accounts for a defined period of time, typically at least every year and accountants spend considerable time at the end of each financial year ensuring that the **final accounts** include only those amounts that relate to a specific financial year. Suppose that you are preparing the profit and loss account for the year ended 31 December 2007. You should include *only* revenue and expenses that relate to 2007 and not include any revenue or expenses relating to matters which should properly be accounted for in 2006 or 2008.

A business which has a year end of 31 December 2007 should include in the profit and loss account only those amounts that relate to the period between 1 January and 31 December 2007. Therefore, if you are preparing the final accounts for the business, you should *not* include any expenses that were incurred or relate to any time *before* 1 January 2007 or *after* 31 December 2007.

Likewise, if an expense, such as the rent of an office, was paid 12 months in advance on the 1 October 2007, then *only* three months of the rent expense (1 October 2007 to 31 December 2007) will be relevant for inclusion in the profit and loss account for the year ending 31 December 2007.

EXAMPLE   Adjustment for accruals (accrued items)

The trial balance of a business shows the computer repairs account as a **debit** balance of £240 as at 31 December 2007. This amount is the total the business has actually paid at the balance sheet date. However, at 31 December 2007 the business has just had another computer repaired but has not yet paid the account amounting to £90. Let us assume that the bill for £90 will be paid sometime in January 2008.

Since you are preparing the profit and loss account for the year ending 31 December 2007, you must include the cost of computer repairs of £90 even though you have not yet paid the account. In other words, you are including all expenses that related to the year ended 31 December 2007 including any expenses that have been incurred but not yet paid. This means you will have to add the £90 outstanding account to the £240 already shown in the trial balance i.e. £330 is now entered into the profit and loss account as an expense.

> Remember that the £90 account has not yet been paid, so it is outstanding and therefore treated as a liability at the accounting year end. In the balance sheet, you should show this accrued (or outstanding) item of £90 as a **current liability**.

We are now in a position to draw up the 'T' **account** for computer repairs as follows:

Computer repairs account

		£			£
31/12/07	Bank	240			
31/12/07	Balance c/f	<u>90</u>	31/12/07	Profit and loss a/c	<u>330</u>
		<u>330</u>			<u>330</u>
			01/01/08	Balance b/f	90

EXAMPLE   Adjustment for prepayment (payment in advance)

Some expenses of a business are paid in advance such as rent or insurance premiums. A business has a year end of 31 October 2007 and on 1 September 2007, the business pays its annual buildings insurance premium of £2,400. The premium relates to an insurance policy which covers the business for the period from 1 September 2007 until 31 August

2008. Although the premium was paid in the accounting year ended 31 October 2007, it is clear that most of the £2,400 actually relates to the next accounting year end, that is the year ended 31 October 2008. Because the annual insurance premium is £2,400 we can see that the insurance cost to the business is £200 per month (that is £2,400 ÷ 12). In other words, only £400 (two months) of the insurance premium of £2,400 relates to the year ended 31 October 2007, while the remaining £2,000 relates to the accounting year ended 31 October 2008.

We can therefore calculate the amount of the prepayment as at 31 October 2007. But in order to calculate the appropriate write off in the profit and loss account for the year ended 31 October 2007, we need to find out if there was a similar prepayment at the end of the previous financial year. Let us assume that there was a prepayment on the buildings insurance account at the 31 October 2006 of £1,600. The £1,600 prepayment at 31 October 2006 must represent 10 months of insurance cover which is equivalent to £160 per month (that is £1,600 ÷ 10). The 'T' account will appear as follows:

Buildings insurance acount

		£			£
01/11/06	Balance b/f	1,600	31/10/07	Profit and loss a/c	2,000
01/09/07	Bank	2,400	31/10/07	Balance c/f	2,000
		4,000			4,000
01/11/07	Balance b/f	2,000			

Note that the amount written off to the profit and loss account is £2,000. We can check that this figure is correct if we remember that the expense for the year ended 31 October 2007 is made up of 10 months at £160 per month (£1,600) *plus* 2 months at £200 per month (£400) making a grand total of £2,000.

> Remember that the £2,000 prepayment has value to the business and should therefore be treated as an **asset** at the accounting year end. In the balance sheet, you should show this prepayment as a **current asset**.

In some cases it is possible for a single account to combine both accruals and prepayments. For instance in the case of motor expenses some items such as vehicle licence duty will be paid a year in advance, while other expenses, such as fuel may be paid in arrears. In the case of telephone services, the provider will charge a line rental (payable in advance) as well as charging for calls (which are paid in arrears once the number, duration and type of calls have been determined and billed).

EXAMPLE QUESTION

Account combining accruals and prepayments

A business whose accounting year end is 31 December 2007 had the following balances on its telephone account at 1 January 2007:

	£
Accrual – call charges for the period 01/12/06 to 31/12/06	<u>210</u>
Prepayment – line rental (two months) paid in advance for the period 01/01/07 to 28/02/07	<u>130</u>

During 2007 the business paid invoices amounting to £3,150. At 31 December 2007 line rental (paid in advance for the period 01/01/08 to 29/02/08) amounted to £145. In addition, call charges which were made during December 2007, but not billed until 2008, were estimated at £260.

Required

Draw up the 'T' account for telephone services for the year ended 31 December 2007.

Solution

For this particular problem we are required to calculate the charge for telephone services which will appear in the profit and loss account for the year ended 31 December 2007. In order to calculate the profit and loss account charge for 2007, it is helpful to draw up a 'T' account for telephone services as follows:

Telephone services account

		£			£
01/01/07	Balance b/f	130	01/01/07	Balance b/f	210
	Bank	3,150	31/12/07	Profit and loss a/c	3,185
31/12/07	Balance c/f	260	31/12/07	Balance c/f	145
		3,540			3,540
01/01/08	Balance b/f	145	01/01/08	Balance b/f	260

At the year end (31 December 2007) the prepayment of £145 should be shown as a current asset in the balance sheet while the accrual of £260 should be shown as a current liability.

Textbook guide

BRITTON AND WATERSTON: *Chapter 5*
JONES: *Chapter 3*

4	
stock valuation	

UK accounting standards refer to **stock** whereas international accounting standards refer to **inventory**. However, both terms have the same meaning. Calculation of an appropriate stock valuation is crucial for two reasons:

1 It determines the valuation of the closing stock in the year end balance sheet. This will affect the total for reported assets.

2 It determines the amount that will be charged as cost of sales in the profit and loss account. This will affect the level of reported profit.

The 'lower of cost and net realisable value' rule means that we can normally expect to value **closing stock** according to its original cost (that is, the amount that was paid for it). Net realisable value would only be used if some deterioration had taken place, which meant that it could only be sold at a selling price lower than the original cost. Few firms would survive for long if this happened on a regular basis.

The most common methods of valuing stock are:

1 **FIFO** (first in first out)

2 **LIFO** (last in first out)

3 **AVCO** (average cost)

But why is there a need for three different methods? Surely a firm should know what it paid for its stock?

The problem is that life is not so simple. Modern commercial practices mean that a company could purchase the same type of item at many different times during the year. Customers will receive some goods as sales and those goods will be replaced. But by the end of the year the firm's stock will contain a mixture of goods bought at different times during the year (and probably at different prices, which is the critical point). When stock items are virtually identical, trying to attach original costs to these items is an unproductive use of time and effort. Instead, firms prefer to make assumptions about how stock items flow through the firm. In other words, assumptions are made about which items went out to customers and which items were retained (as closing stock) at the year end.

We can illustrate the differences between FIFO, LIFO and AVCO in the following worked example.

EXAMPLE

An electrical store opened on 1 July and included light bulbs in its stock for sale. All purchases take place on the first day of the month and sales take place during the month. During the three months to 30 September, the following purchases and sales were made:

	Unit purchases	Unit cost (p)	Cost of purchases (£)	Unit sales
July	600	30	180	400
August	720	35	252	800
September	900	40	360	850
	2,220		792	2,050

We now have all the information we need to calculate the value of closing stock at 30 September under the following rules:

1 FIFO

2 LIFO

3 AVCO

For these types of question it is useful to have in mind a clear procedure for tracing the items of stock as they enter and leave the firm. The following table helps to attach the assumed purchase price to the relevant stock items. Remember that, for the time being, we are concerned only with the purchase price. We are ignoring the selling price (we can come on to that later). For now, when we talk about sales we are interested only in unit sales or the cost of the stock items which made up those sales.

> *In an exam you can use the table to work methodically through the question. If you do make a mistake, you will have a better chance of correcting it. If you do not spot your mistake, there is a better chance that the examiner will be able to follow your workings and you may still get most of the marks, provided your method is sound.*

FIFO

FIFO makes the assumption that the oldest items brought into stock, will be first to go out to satisfy sales.

Purchase price	30p Units	35p Units	40p Units	Total
July purchases	600			600
July sales	(400)			(400)
End July	200			200
August purchases		720		720
August sales	(200)	(600)		(800)
End August	–	120		120
September purchases			900	900
September sales	——	(120)	(730)	(850)
End September	==	==	170	170

We can calculate that the closing stock consists entirely of 170 items purchased during September at a unit cost of 40p. Therefore the closing stock on the FIFO basis is valued at $170 \times 40p = £68.00$.

LIFO

LIFO makes the assumption that the most recent items brought into stock, will be first to go out to satisfy sales.

Purchase price	30p Units	35p Units	40p Units	Total
July purchases	600			600
July sales	(400)			(400)
End July	200			200
August purchases		720		720
August sales	(80)	(720)		(800)
End August	120	–		120
September purchases			900	900
September sales	——	——	(850)	(850)
End September	120	==	50	170

We can calculate that the closing stock consists entirely of 120 items purchased during July at a unit cost of 30p, and 50 items purchased during September at a unit cost of 40p. Therefore the closing stock on the LIFO basis is valued at (120 × 30p) + (50 × 40p) = £56.00.

We can now see clearly the difference between FIFO and LIFO. FIFO makes the fairly reasonable assumption that the firm will try to use up its oldest stock first. LIFO makes the rather unusual assumption that a firm will send out its most recent stock to customers, meaning that it could be carrying stock which was bought a long time ago.

Remember that FIFO and LIFO are only assumptions about how the firm is presumed to act, and the reality, in fact, may be quite different from these assumptions.

AVCO

Finally, we can consider the average cost method, or AVCO. Under AVCO, a weighted average cost is calculated. The average cost is recalculated whenever the price changes.

	Units	Unit price (p)	Stock value (£)	Average cost per unit (p)
July purchases	600	30.000	180.00	
July sales	(400)		(120.00)	
End July	200		60.00	30.000
August purchases	720	35.000	252.00	
	920		312.00	33.913
August sales	(800)	33.913	(271.30)	
	120		40.70	
September purchases	900	40.000	360.00	
	1,020		400.70	39.284
September sales	(850)	39.284	333.92	
End September	170		66.78	

The firm is left with 170 units in stock. Given an average cost of 39.284p per unit at the end of September, the stock value is 170 × 39.284 = £66.78.

It is important to consider what happens as stock price changes over a financial period. In the UK we are used to prices of most items increasing over time. But this is not always the case. Prices of many electronic goods have actually been falling over time. But if we consider what happens if prices have been increasing, we can readily see that, under FIFO assumptions, the closing stock valuation will be relatively high, because we are assuming that most of the stock was purchased recently (at the higher price). On the other hand, under LIFO assumptions, the closing stock valuation will be relatively low, because we are assuming that much of the stock was bought a long time ago when prices were lower. As you might guess, stock valuation under the average cost method will tend to fall in between FIFO and LIFO.

You should be prepared for a question which might ask you what happens if the purchase price of stock is decreasing over time. The above assumptions are then reversed, so that FIFO will give a relatively low valuation, because we are assuming that most of the stock was purchased recently at the lower price. But, under LIFO assumptions, the stock valuation will be relatively high, because we are assuming that much of the stock was bought a long time ago when prices were higher.

So far we have considered only the implications for the valuation of stock in the balance sheet. Let's now consider what the implications are for the profit and loss account. We need to remember that closing stock is an important item in the calculation of cost of goods sold in the profit and loss account. Let us now see what happens to the profit and loss account when we use these three different assumptions, and to make it more realistic we will assume that the unit selling price was 60p in all three months.

The relevant section of the profit and loss account will be as follows:

	FIFO	LIFO	AVCO
	£	£	£
Sales (2,050 × 60p)	1,230	1,230	1,230
Purchases	892	892	892
Less closing stock	**68**	**56**	**67**
Cost of goods sold	824	836	825
Gross profit	406	394	405

The prices which the firm paid for its purchases of stock have been increasing over the period. But note that whichever of the three assumptions we use, sales revenue and cost of purchases remains the same. However, the different assumptions for stock valuation mean that closing stock value is different in each case and this affects the figure for cost of goods sold and in turn gross profit is affected.

To summarise, FIFO gives a high value for closing stock, a low figure for cost of goods sold and a high figure for gross profit. LIFO gives the opposite – a low value for closing stock, a high figure for cost of goods sold and a low figure for gross profit. AVCO (as we might expect) lies somewhere between the two.

Why then is stock valuation important? It is important because, when prices change, LIFO and FIFO can give us different gross profit figures in the profit and loss account, and different values for stock in the balance sheet.

You might ask why some companies don't choose LIFO because if they did they would then pay lower **tax** on their (lower) reported profits. This is an interesting issue. In the US companies are allowed under certain circumstances to use the LIFO method and some do. This can be helpful in reducing the tax they pay to the government. There is a definite cash flow benefit to these companies because their tax payments are reduced. On the other hand the value of stock in the balance sheet is likely to be out of date since it will reflect stock bought in the past. But in the UK, the government does not allow LIFO and in fact LIFO is not permitted under UK and international accounting standards.

EXAMPLE QUESTION

A garden centre opened for trade on 1 May 2007. Included in its product lines is a particular type of clay pot. During May 2007 the garden centre purchases the following quantities from its supplier.

Date	Quantity	Unit price
5 May	160	£12
14 May	70	£21
23 May	35	£14

In the same month, sales were made as follows:

Date	Quantity
10 May	105
17 May	75
26 May	30

Required

Calculate the closing stock value for May 2007 assuming that:

1 the FIFO method of stock valuation is used;

2 the LIFO method of stock valuation is used.

Solution to question

1 FIFO method of stock valuation

Purchase price	£12 Units	£21 Units	£14 Units	Total
5 May purchases	160			160
10 May sales	(105)			(105)
	55			55
14 May purchases		70		70
17 May sales	(55)	(20)		(75)
	–	50		50
23 May purchases			35	35
26 May sales		(30)		(30)
End May		20	35	55

The closing stock on the FIFO basis is calculated as:

$$(20 \times £21) + (35 \times £14) = £910$$

2 LIFO method of stock valuation

Purchase price	£12 *Units*	£21 *Units*	£14 *Units*	*Total*
5 May purchases	160			160
10 May sales	(105)			(105)
	55			55
14 May purchases		70		70
17 May sales	(5)	(70)		(75)
	50	–		50
23 May purchases			35	35
26 May sales			(30)	(30)
End May	50	==	5	55

The closing stock on the LIFO basis is calculated as:

$$(50 \times £12) + (5 \times £14) = £670$$

Textbook guide

ATRILL AND MCLANEY: *Chapter 3*
BRITTON AND WATERSTON: *Chapter 3*
HAND, ISAAKS AND SANDERSON: *Chapter 5*

5	
bad and doubtful debts	

When you are preparing the financial statements for a business, you will frequently find reference to bad and doubtful debts. Examiners often assess this topic with a practical question or occasionally by a short written question.

It is important to ensure you understand the difference between **bad debts** and **doubtful debts**.

Bad debts

Bad debts are incurred when it is reasonably certain that a debtor to a business will not be paying. For example the debtor's business may itself have collapsed – leaving no funds in which to pay its obligations. You should treat bad debts in the same manner as any other expense.

For example, if the trial balance shows a debit entry for bad debts of £700 then treat this £700 as an expense and enter this figure in the profit and loss account. (You do not need to make a balance sheet adjustment to debtors because the debtors' figure in the trial balance will already have had the bad debts subtracted.)

EXAMPLE   Treatment of bad debts in the accounts

At the 31 December 2007 a business has debtors amounting to £73,200. It has identified two customers owing £3,400 and £2,360 who both went into liquidation in the last six months. It is believed that neither of these two amounts or any part of them will be recovered from the liquidators. How would this information be recorded in the accounts of the business?

First we need to recognise that the debtors' figure of £73,200 will need to be adjusted since it would be incorrect to show that valuation in the balance sheet.

Balance sheet (extract)

	£
Debtors	73,200
Less specific bad debts written off to profit and loss a/c	5,760
Net debtors (included in current assets)	67,440

Next we need to note that the profit figure will be reduced due to the impact of the bad debt on the financial performance of the business.

Profit and loss account (extract)

	£
Bad debts written off	5,760

It is important to realise that bad debts, once written off, no longer form a part of the double entry bookkeeping system. Nevertheless the business would be well advised to keep a record of this information, because it sometimes happens that an administrator is able to pay a **dividend** (that is, some of the outstanding debts) to the creditors of a failed business, in some cases years after the business failed.

Doubtful debts

However, in addition to bad debts you may also be required to account for doubtful debts. In practice, businesses have learnt from experience that some debtors will not pay – but they are not certain which debtors this applies to at the end of the year. Businesses have to make a judgement on what proportion of debtors might not pay. For example, some businesses operate in sectors of the economy which carry a higher risk of failure compared to other sectors of the economy. In the catering or building sectors it might be prudent to assume that a relatively high proportion of debtors should be classified as 'doubtful'. In contrast, businesses that have debtors in a much safer and less risky sector – such as in the government sector – might need to classify a smaller proportion as 'doubtful'.

The following example illustrates how you show a **provision for doubtful debts** in the profit and loss account and balance sheet.

EXAMPLE   Provision for doubtful debts

The opening provision for doubtful debts as shown in the trial balance at 1 January 2007 is £1,000. If no adjustment is made to this figure then at the end of the year on 31 December 2007 there will still be a £1,000 provision. The provision for doubtful debts of £1,000 means that the business has estimated that £1,000 worth of debtors might not pay their obligations.

However it might be that the trading circumstances of those debtors change over the course of the year, which means that debtors might be more or less likely to pay up.

> *Make sure you understand why the size of the provision can change over time. Firstly, it can change because the trading environment has improved or worsened. Secondly the size of the provision can change simply because the business has grown in size and you would therefore expect it to carry a larger amount of debtors. We would consequently expect the size of the provision to increase also.*

Check the notes that you are normally provided with at the bottom of the trial balance.

(a) Increase in provision for doubtful debts

A typical note at the bottom of the trial balance might read:

> The provision for doubtful debts is to be increased to 3% of debtors.

Next you need to go to the trial balance and find the debtors' balance, and let us assume that it is £60,000.

We now have all the information we need to calculate the increase in the provision for the year ended 31 December 2007, as well as the amount of the provision at 31 December 2007.

Firstly we can calculate the size of the provision at 31 December 2007:

$$3\% \times £60,000 = £1,800.$$

Remember that the business has already included a provision in the trial balance of £1,000, which means you have to *increase* the provision for doubtful debts by £800 (that is, £1,800 – £1,000).

Since this £800 is an *increase* you must remember to enter this £800 increase in the profit and loss account for year ending 31 December 2007 as an **expense**.

If you are unsure about how the entries should be recorded, it is always helpful to draw up a 'T' account.

The other side of the credit entry of £800 in the provision for doubtful debts account will be a debit entry of £800 in the profit and loss account.

Provision for doubtful debts account

		£			£
			01/01/07	Balance b/f	1,000
31/12/07	Balance c/f	1,800	31/12/07	Profit and loss a/c	800
		1,800			1,800
			01/01/08	Balance b/f	1,800

(b) Decrease in provision for doubtful debts

On the other hand it is quite possible that we are asked to reduce the provision for doubtful debts.

Suppose that the note at the bottom of the trial balance instead reads:

The provision for doubtful debts is to be reduced to 1% of debtors.

Now we can calculate the size of the provision at 31 December 2007:

$$1\% \times £60,000 = £600.$$

Remember that the business has included a provision in the trial balance of £1,000 (which was based on the level of debtors at the start of the financial year), so you have to *decrease* the provision for doubtful debts by £400 (that is, £1,000 − £600).

Since this £400 is a *decrease* you must remember to enter this £400 amount to the profit and loss account for year ending 31 December 2007. The figure of £400 will actually improve the reported profit of the business and is treated as a credit entry and therefore *added back* to **gross profit**.

Provision for doubtful debts account

		£			£
31/12/07	Profit and loss a/c	400			
31/12/07	Balance c/f	600	01/01/07	Balance b/f	1,000
		1,000			1,000
			01/01/08	Balance b/f	600

The other side of the debit entry of £400 in the provision for doubtful debts account will be a credit entry of £400 in the profit and loss account.

Try to get into the habit of thinking of increases in profit as 'good news' and decreases in profit as 'bad news'. So an increase in the doubtful debt provision is intuitively 'bad news' because it means that the firm will be able to recover less money from its debtors. On the other hand, a decrease in the doubtful debt provision is intuitively 'good news' because it means that the firm will be able to recover more money from its debtors.

Next you need to understand how a provision for doubtful debts is treated in the balance sheet. You must *subtract* the whole of the newly calculated provision for doubtful debts from the debtors' balance (and *not* just the increase or the decrease in the provision).

So in the example (a) earlier, the balance sheet entries for debtors as at 31 December 2007 would be:

	£
Debtors	60,000
Less provision for doubtful debts	1,800
Net debtors (included in current assets)	58,200

Note that the figure of £1,800 consists of the original provision of £1,000 *plus* the increase in the provision of £800.

And in the example (b) above, the balance sheet entries for debtors as at 31 December 2007 would be:

	£
Debtors	60,000
Less provision for doubtful debts	600
Net debtors (included in current assets)	59,400

Note that the figure of £600 consists of the original provision of £1,000 *minus* the decrease in the provision of £400.

EXAMPLE QUESTION

Bad debts combined with provision for doubtful debts

At 31 December 2006, a business had debtors amounting to £43,000 and a general provision for doubtful debts calculated as 2 per cent of debtors. At 31 December 2007 the business had on its books debtors amounting to £62,500. Included in this figure were amounts owing (£3,500) from specific customers who had been identified as 'bad' and would need to be written off. Due to the worsening financial and economic environment during 2007, the business had decided to increase its general provision for doubtful debts to 3 per cent.

You are required to calculate:

(a) the bad debt write off in the profit and loss account in 2007;

(b) the reported figure of debtors in the balance sheet at the end of the financial year;

(c) the change in provision for doubtful debts in 2007;

(d) the total expense charged to profit and loss account for bad debts and provision for doubtful debts in 2007.

Suggested answer

(a)   The bad debt write-off in the profit and loss account in 2007
The bad debt write-off in the profit and loss account in 2007 is simply the specific debts which have been identified as 'bad' by the business and which can be eliminated from the bookkeeping system. These, as we are told, total £3,500.

(b)   The reported figure of debtors in the balance sheet at the end of the financial year
Next we need to calculate the provision for doubtful debts which will be required at 31 December 2007. But we have to remember that the specific bad debts (£3,500) are eliminated from the accounting records of the business. Therefore the general provision for doubtful debts will be calculated on the debtors' figure at 31 December 2007 *minus* the specific bad debts written off.

	£
Debtors	62,500
Less specific bad debts written off	3,500
	59,000
Less provision for doubtful debts (3% × £59,000)	1,770
Debtors (as per balance sheet at 31 December 2007)	57,230

(c)   The change in provision for doubtful debts in 2007

We need to calculate the size of the provision at the beginning of 2007. From the information given we can see that the provision amounted to £860 (that is £43,000 × 2%).

We now have all the information we need to calculate the change in provision for doubtful debts in 2007. The information can be set out in 'T' account form as follows:

Provision for doubtful debts account

		£			£
			01/01/07	Balance b/f	860
31/12/07	Balance c/f	1,770	31/12/07	Profit and loss a/c	910
		1,770			1,770
			01/01/08	Balance b/f	1,770

(d)   The total expense charged to profit and loss account for bad debts and provision for doubtful debts in 2007

The total expense charged in the profit and loss account for the year ended 31 December 2007 consists of the specific bad debt write off plus the increase in the provision for doubtful debts:

	£
Specific bad debts written off	3,500
Increase in provision for doubtful debts	910
Total profit and loss a/c expense for bad and doubtful debts	4,410

The calculation of an appropriate figure for debtors in the year end balance sheet represents one of the major challenges to accountants. It is a good example of why reported accounting figures under the accruals accounting system do not represent 'facts' but incorporate estimates. When a business calculates its doubtful debt provision it is trying in effect to estimate the likelihood that its customers will pay up at some future date. Accruals accounting, therefore, can be subject to bias and the danger is that companies whose financial performance is poor may find it convenient to underestimate the level of problem debts and thereby enhance the reported profit figure. On the other hand, it is vital for investors, banks and others that companies publish accounting information which is consistent with economic reality. It is therefore the task of accountants and auditors to ensure that provisions for doubtful debts are calculated as objectively as possible.

Textbook guide

ATRILL AND MCLANEY: *Chapter 3*
BRITTON AND WATERSTON: *Chapter 6*
JONES: *Chapter 6*

6	
fixed assets and depreciation	

Depreciation

The fixed assets of a business will usually be purchased in one accounting period but will normally last for many future years. These fixed assets, consisting of items such as buildings, computers, plant and machinery, etc. will be used in the business to generate future earnings for many years, and in the case of buildings, perhaps for many decades. Legally and also in accordance with accounting standards, the cost of an asset must be allocated over the period of time expected to benefit from its use. The UK accounting standard *FRS 15, Tangible Fixed Assets*, states that the fundamental objective of depreciation is to reflect in the **operating profit** the cost of using tangible fixed assets. In other words, when a company uses a fixed asset, it is consuming economic resources and these should be reflected in the financial statements during the useful economic life of the asset. The relevant international accounting standard, *IAS 16, Property, Plant and Equipment*, defines depreciation as 'the systematic allocation of the depreciable amount of an asset over its useful life'. Depreciable amount is simply the amount to be depreciated, that is, the cost of the asset less its residual scrap value.

Remember: depreciation should be allocated to accounting periods so as to charge a fair proportion to each accounting period during the expected useful life of the asset. In the assessment and allocation of depreciation to accounting periods, there are three key factors that need to be considered:

1. cost (or valuation – if the asset has been revalued);

2. nature of the asset and the length of its expected useful life to the business, having due regard to the incidence of obsolescence;

3. estimated residual (or scrap) value.

In a conceptual sense, depreciation attempts to ensure that a company does not deplete its capital base. So if a company does not provide for depreciation of its fixed assets in its profit and loss account, the company's earnings will, in relative terms, be overstated. If the earnings are overstated by not providing for depreciation, then, excessively high levels of profits (or dividends) could be taken out of the business. As a result, the accounting danger is that profits and dividends are distributed from the capital base of the business, which in effect depletes the capital of the business.

To assist in maintaining the capital base of a business, it is important that a provision is made for the depreciation of the fixed assets that were originally acquired. The accounting process of making this provision is by including a depreciation charge in the profit and loss account of the business.

It is most important to realise that the depreciation concept is not designed to provide a means or method to replace ageing assets. Depreciation is not intended to be a 'savings-scheme' by which the company can fund purchases of new assets. Many non-accountants believe that depreciation creates a fund which will provide for the purchase of new investment in the future. On the contrary, the purpose of depreciation is to maintain the original capital base of the company by acting as a constraint on the amount of profits available for distribution as dividends. If a business is concerned about replacing its existing fixed assets in the future, it will need to set aside some of its current profits in order to fund the future asset purchases.

We can now consider the three most common **depreciation** *methods* which are:

1 straight line method;

2 reducing balance method (or sometimes termed the diminishing balance method);

3 sum of years' digits method.

1 Straight line method

Under this commonly used method of depreciation, an equal charge for depreciation is entered into the profit and loss account each year. This method can be illustrated by the following formula:

$$\text{Annual depreciation charge (to profit and loss account)} = \frac{\text{Original cost (or value) of fixed asset} - \text{estimated residual (scrap) value}}{\text{Estimated useful economic life (years)}}$$

In the balance sheet of the business, the fixed asset will be shown at its net amount (i.e. less depreciation).

For example, Company ABC Plc has an accounting year end of 31 December and it purchased a machine for £10,000 in 2007. It decides that the machine has a useful life of 4 years, with a scrap value of £2,000.

In the profit and loss account, the depreciation charge every year from 2007 to 2010 will be £2,000, which is calculated as:

$$\frac{£10,000 - £2,000}{4 \text{ years}}$$

In the balance sheet, the machine would be shown as:

Date	Cost (£)	Depreciation (£)	Net book value (£)
31 December 2007	10,000	2,000	8,000
31 December 2008	10,000	4,000	6,000
31 December 2009	10,000	6,000	4,000
31 December 2010	10,000	8,000	2,000

Note that the depreciation figure shown in the above table is the accumulated depreciation and not simply the depreciation for a given year. So, for example, the £6,000 depreciation balance figure as at 31 December 2009 comprises the annual depreciation in 2007 plus the annual depreciation in 2008 plus the annual depreciation in 2009.

As can be seen from the table above an advantage of the straight line method for many companies is that it is simple to apply. On the other hand, its simplicity means that it is less likely to accord with 'economic reality' or the way in which we normally think assets behave (or lose value) over time.

> Remember it is often normal business practice to include a full year's depreciation in the year an asset is acquired – even if the asset is acquired towards the end of the financial year. But on the other hand, it is normal practice not to include depreciation in the year of disposal. If this topic arises in an exam question, then read the information in the question carefully to see if this practice applies in the question. If the question does not refer to any practice then state your assumption – such as indicated above.

2 Reducing balance method (sometimes termed the diminishing balance method)

The reducing balance method is sometimes described as an accelerated method. Under this method, a fixed percentage rate of depreciation charge is applied to the fixed assets. The actual percentage charge can be mathematically calculated, although many companies choose to use a reasonably practical percentage figure for calculation. The particular percentage used will depend on their own experience of the types of assets used by the business. Each year's depreciation charge in the profit and loss account will vary in size and become progressively less as the years pass. The idea that depreciation charges will reduce over time has some intuitive appeal. For instance, we can imagine that a brand new car will lose a substantial amount of its 'value' in the first year after purchase. But subsequently, even though the value of the car will reduce, the annual amount of this reduction will not be as great as it was in the first year after purchase. An advantage, therefore, of the reducing balance method is that it seems to accord more with 'economic reality' than does the straight line method. On the other hand it is more complicated to apply in practice.

The depreciation rate on the reducing balance method can be calculated mathematically, using the following formula:

$$r = 1 - \sqrt[n]{\frac{s}{c}}$$

where:

r = annual depreciation rate
n = years of useful life
s = scrap or residual value
c = recorded cost

Using the same data as in the straight line method, we can calculate the annual depreciation rate (r):

$$r = 1 - \sqrt[4]{\frac{2,000}{10,000}}$$

$$r = 1 - 0.6687 = 33.13\%$$

We can now apply the calculated depreciation rate of 33.13 per cent as follows:

In the profit and loss account, the entries would be:

Year end	Depreciation (£)	Calculated as
31 December 2007	3,313	33.13% of £10,000
31 December 2008	2,215	33.13% of £6,687 (i.e. £10,000 – £3,313)
31 December 2009	1,481	33.13% of £4,472 (i.e. £6,687 – £2,215)
31 December 2010	991	33.13% of £2,991 (i.e. £4,472 – £1,482)

In the balance sheet, the machine would be recorded as:

Date	Cost (£)	Depreciation (£)	Net book value (£)
31 December 2007	10,000	3,313	6,687
31 December 2008	10,000	5,528	4,472
31 December 2009	10,000	7,009	2,991
31 December 2010	10,000	8,000	2,000

3 Sum of years' digits

The sum of years' digits method is (like the reducing balance method) an accelerated method of depreciation; that is, the charges to the profit and loss account in the earlier years are heavier than in the later years. You are also likely to find an understanding of this method useful since it is an accepted method for apportioning interest charges over the life of a leased asset. Although leasing is not covered in this book, it is quite likely that you will encounter it in more advanced accounting courses. As an example of how the sum of years' digits method is used, let us take the data from the last example of the reducing balance method:

Let us suppose that Company ABC purchases a machine in 2007 for £10,000, which will have a useful life of four years and at 31 December 2010 it is estimated that the machine will have a scrap value of £2,000. The depreciable amount is £8,000 (that is, £10,000 − £2,000) and it is allocated to each year based on a proportion calculated as the number of years remaining divided by the sum of the years. The sum of the years (the denominator in the equation) is $4 + 3 + 2 + 1 = 10$. In the first year the numerator is 4, for the second year it is 3 and so on.

In the profit and loss account, the entries would be:

Year end	Depreciation (£)	Calculated as
31 December 2007	3,200	$4/10 \times £8,000$
31 December 2008	2,400	$3/10 \times £8,000$
31 December 2009	1,600	$2/10 \times £8,000$
31 December 2010	800	$1/10 \times £8,000$

In the balance sheet, the machine would be recorded as:

Date	Cost (£)	Depreciation (£)	Net book value (£)
31 December 2007	10,000	3,200	6,400
31 December 2008	10,000	5,600	4,400
31 December 2009	10,000	7,200	2,800
31 December 2010	10,000	8,000	2,000

Summary

It is interesting to compare the outcomes under the three different depreciation methods. What is noticeable is that although the depreciation charges are different in each of the years 2007 through to 2010, the total depreciation charge for the four years is identical. It is important to understand that depreciation is simply a method of allocating a suitable charge to the profit and loss account over time. As was stated earlier, depreciation helps to ensure that the original capital base of the company is maintained by reducing the amount of profits available for distribution as dividends.

Depreciation charge in profit and loss account for year ended	Straight line	Reducing balance	Sum of years' digits
	£	£	£
31 December 2007	2,000	3,313	3,200
31 December 2008	2,000	2,215	2,400
31 December 2009	2,000	1,481	1,600
31 December 2010	2,000	991	800
Total depreciation	**8,000**	**8,000**	**8,000**

The straight line method is the most straightforward to apply, but it has the disadvantage that it does not seem to reflect the loss in value of a fixed asset over time. The two accelerated methods are reasonably similar and have the advantage of being a closer reflection of 'economic reality'.

Remember also that it is important, when analysing financial statements, to have regard to the company's depreciation policy. The amount of depreciation charged in the profit and loss account and information from the supporting 'notes to the accounts' concerning depreciation methods and policies should be carefully examined. Particularly in the case of land and buildings, the reader should note whether the depreciation is being charged on the original cost of the asset or (in the instance of companies revaluing their fixed assets) on the new revalued figure.

Accounting entries

You should also ensure that you understand that you can produce the underlying 'T' accounts to record depreciation.

EXAMPLE

A Ltd buys a computer for £900 on 1 January 2007. It is expected to last three years and have a nil scrap value at the end of its life. Using the straight line method of depreciation, you are required to record the relevant accounting entries.

Firstly, you will need a computer account and secondly a provision for depreciation account.

Computer account

		£			£
01/01/07	Bank	900	31/12/07	Balance c/f	900
01/01/08	Balance b/f	900	31/12/08	Balance c/f	900
01/01/09	Balance b/f	900	31/12/09	Balance c/f	900

Note the entries stay the same each year. The computer account merely records the original cost of the asset.

Secondly, now produce a 'Provision for depreciation account'. In this account, you will record the amount of depreciation being written off as an expense to the profit and loss account each year. This account will also show the accumulated depreciation on the asset as the years progress.

Since we are depreciating the asset over three years using the straight line basis the amount of annual depreciation to be charged each year is £300.

The formula is:

$$\frac{cost - scrap\ value}{expected\ useful\ life}$$

$$\frac{£900 - Nil}{3\ years} = £300$$

Provision for depreciation account

		£			£
31/12/07	Balance c/f	300	31/12/07	Profit and loss a/c	300
			01/01/08	Balance b/f	300
31/12/08	Balance c/f	600	31/12/08	Profit and loss a/c	300
		600			600
			01/01/09	Balance b/f	600
31/12/09	Balance c/f	900	31/12/09	Profit and loss a/c	300
		900			900

So now, you have all the information you need to enter depreciation as an expense in the profit and loss account and to show the total depreciation in the balance sheet.

For example, in the profit and loss account for the year ending 31 December 2007 the depreciation shown as an expense is £300 and £300 for each of the following two years.

In the balance sheet, the computer will be shown as a fixed asset.

At 31 December 2007 the balance sheet will show:

	Cost (£)	Depreciation (£)	Net book value (£)
Computer	900	300	600

(Note the £300 depreciation figure can be taken direct from the provision for depreciation account above.)

At 31 December 2008 the balance sheet will show:

	Cost (£)	Depreciation (£)	Net book value (£)
Computer	900	600	300

(Do remember that the depreciation column shows the accumulated depreciation since the computer was acquired, i.e. £300 + £300. The original cost figure of £900 stays the same.)

At 31 December 2009, the balance sheet will show:

	Cost (£)	Depreciation (£)	Net book value (£)
Computer	900	900	nil

The computer has now been fully depreciated and is shown as nil in the **net book value** column of the balance sheet.

Sale of fixed assets

You may sometimes find that a business disposes of (or sells) a fixed asset.

It is important to remember *not* to include the receipts from the sale of fixed assets in the 'sales' figure in the trading and profit and loss account.

However, you are required to *include* the *profit on disposal* or *loss on disposal* of fixed assets in the trading and profit and loss account.

This profit or loss on disposal must be calculated as illustrated below:

For instance, in the above example of A Ltd, let us now assume that on 1 January 2008 the company sells the computer for £750 (remember that it acquired the computer on 1 January 2007).

Using the straight line basis, the annual depreciation charge is £300 for the first year (i.e. in 2007).

So in the balance sheet at 31 December 2007 the computer is shown at a net book value of £600 (i.e. £900 – £300).

If the computer is sold on 1 January 2008 for £750 (remember there is no depreciation in the year of sale) then the profit on disposal is £150 (i.e. £750 – £600).

This profit of £150 is then credited back to the gross profit in the trading and profit and loss account.

Recording the entries for profit or loss on disposal of fixed assets

If you prefer, you can record the above entries in 'T' accounts:

Computer (asset) account

		£			£
01/01/07	Bank	900	31/12/07	Balance c/f	900
				Computer	
01/01/08	Balance b/f	900	01/01/08	Disposal a/c	900

Since the computer is disposed of on 1 January 2008, the cost is transferred to another account (called 'computer disposal account'). We therefore credit the computer (asset) account with £900 and we debit the computer disposal account

We also need to consider the issue of depreciation. The original cost of the computer has been removed from the computer (asset) account. So we need to remove the balance on the provision for depreciation account (and transfer the amount of £300 to the computer disposal account).

Provision for depreciation account

		£			£
31/12/07	Balance c/f	300	31/12/07	Profit and loss a/c	300
01/01/08	Computer Disposal a/c	300	01/01/08	Balance b/f	300

Now we are in a position to complete the entries in the computer disposal account.

Computer disposal account

		£			£
31/12/07	Computer a/c	900	01/01/08	Bank	750
				Provision for	
31/12/08	Profit on		01/01/08	Depreciation	
	disposal	150		a/c	300
		1,050			1,050

This £150 profit on disposal is then shown in the profit and loss account.

> It is important to remember that the profit on disposal is not a 'true' trading profit. Rather it has arisen because the original estimated depreciation rate was not accurate. In this sense, it is more accurate to describe a 'profit on disposal' as an 'overprovision for depreciation in previous years', and it would be more meaningful to describe a 'loss on disposal' as an 'underprovision for depreciation in previous years'.

In an examination question you may be asked to discuss the relevance of market values to depreciation. Is it more useful to report market values or historic costs? In this type of question you should always be aware that there are different types of user of information, ranging from investors and lenders through to employees and customers.

You might also be asked to consider whether reducing balance (which gives a valuation closer to market value) is relevant to a company which intends to hold on to an asset for a considerable period of time.

Types of questions

Questions on depreciation are examined very frequently by examiners. You should give this topic your full attention during the course of your revision.

(Continued)

EXAMPLE QUESTION

At 1 January 2007 the following details were taken from the books of Southern Ltd:

	Cost	Accumulated depreciation	Net book value
	(£)	(£)	(£)
Fixtures and fittings	266,500	90,750	175,750
Motor vehicles	147,000	47,530	99,470

In August 2007 a van which originally cost £34,500 in April 2005 was sold for £20,500. In September 2007 an estate car was purchased at a cost of £49,500.

In February 2007 additional shop fittings were purchased at a cost of £23,000 and in November 2007 some office furniture was disposed of for scrap (realising £500). This furniture originally cost £26,900 in June 2001.

Fixtures and fittings are depreciated on the straight line basis at 15 per cent per annum. Motor vehicles are depreciated on the declining balance basis at 25 per cent per annum. It is company policy to provide a full year's depreciation on assets in the year of purchase but to provide no depreciation in the year of sale or disposal.

Required

Show how the above information would be recorded in the books of Southern Ltd for the year ended 31 December 2007. Your answer should include the relevant asset and depreciation accounts, a disposals account and extracts from the profit and loss account.

Suggested answer

Fixtures and fittings (asset) account

		£			£
01/01/07	Balance b/f	266,500		Disposal a/c	26,900
	Additions at cost	23,000	31/12/07	Balance c/f	262,600
		289,500			289,500
01/01/08	Balance b/f	262,600			

Motor vehicles (asset) account

		£			£
01/01/07	Balance b/f	147,000		Disposal a/c	34,500
	Additions at cost	49,500	31/12/07	Balance c/f	
		196,500			162,000
					196,500
01/01/08	Balance b/f	162,000			

Fixtures and fittings provision for depreciation account

		£			£
			01/01/07	Balance b/f	90,750
	Disposal a/c			Profit and loss a/c	
	(Note 2)	24,210		(Note 1)	39,390
31/12/07	Balance c/f	105,930			
		130,140			130,140
			01/01/08	Balance b/f	105,930

Motor vehicles provision for depreciation account

		£				£
			01/01/07	Balance b/f		47,530
	Disposal a/c			Profit and loss a/c		
	(Note 3)	15,090		(Note 4)		32,390
31/12/07	Balance c/f	64,830				
		79,920				79,920
			01/01/08	Balance b/f		64,830

Fixed assets disposal account

	£		£
Fixtures and fittings cost	26,900	Fixtures and fittings depreciation	24,210
Motor vehicles cost	34,500	Motor vehicles depreciation	15,090
Profit on disposal	1,090	Fixtures and fittings scrap – cash	500
Motor vehicles			
		Motor vehicles sale – cash	20,500
		Loss on disposal	
		– Fixtures and fittings	2,190
	62,490		62,490

Notes

1 £39,390 = 15% × £262,600

2 £26,900 depreciated for 6 years @ 15% = £24,210

3 £34,500 depreciated for 2 years @ 25% = £15,090

4 £32,390 = 25% × (£162,000 − £32,440)

Profit and loss account (extracts)

	£
Fixtures and fittings depreciation	39,390
Loss on disposal	2,190
	41,580
Motor vehicles depreciation	32,390
Profit on disposal	1,090
	31,300

Textbook guide

ATRILL AND MCLANEY: *Chapter 3*
BRITTON AND WATERSTON: *Chapter 6*
HAND, ISAAKS AND SANDERSON: *Chapter 5*
JONES: *Chapter 5*

7	
the balance sheet	

Most accounting examinations will contain a question that includes a balance sheet (as well as a profit and loss account) and you should thoroughly understand this topic.

A balance sheet is a list of a business's assets, liabilities and equity at a given point in time. You may often see a balance sheet typically described as a photograph or 'snap shot' of a business at a specific day and time.

Assets

The balance sheet will show two types of assets:

Fixed assets

Fixed assets (also referred to as 'non-current assets') include items such as factories, machinery, office buildings, computers, furniture, vehicles, etc. These types of assets are intended to be used to help the business generate revenue over a period of time. Normally these categories of assets will need to be depreciated. (See the previous section which deals with fixed assets and depreciation.)

Current assets

These types of assets are constantly changing and include stock, debtors, bank and cash. They are sometimes referred to as 'circulating assets' since a major objective of a business is to buy stock, which it converts into debtors (as a result of sales to customers). When the customers eventually pay cash, the debtors are converted into cash and the cycle can begin again.

Other categories of fixed assets

Assets are categorised in another way such as **tangible** and **intangible** **assets**.

Tangible assets are assets with a solid physical presence such as buildings, machinery and computer printers.

Intangible assets are 'abstract' assets that do not have a physical presence. Examples of intangible assets are trademarks, licences, computer software and **goodwill**.

Liabilities

There are two categories of liabilities which are included in the balance sheet.

Current liabilities

Current liabilities are the short term obligations of the firm and include amounts owing to trade creditors (who have supplied goods on credit) and expenses which have not yet been paid (such as electricity, telecommunication services).

Long term liabilities

Long term liabilities (sometimes called 'non-current liabilities') refer to obligations where the payment is further into the future. A typical example would be a bank loan which is repayable in several years' time.

As a general rule, current liabilities are normally considered to be those which fall due for payment within one year of the balance sheet date. Long term liaibilites are those which fall due for payment more than one year from the balance sheet date.

In the balance sheet, the categories of *fixed assets* and **current assets** are added together to give a subtotal of *total assets*. Next are deducted **current liabilities**, then *long term liabilities* are deducted to give a final total of **net assets**. The figure of net assets is the balance sheet total. This balance sheet total is identical in amount to the total equity.

Equity

Equity refers to the interest of the owner(s) in the business. The equity interest is expressed differently depending on whether a sole trader or company with limited liability is being considered. But, in principle, the concept of equity is no different for a sole trader or a shareholder.

In the case of a sole trader, equity consists of the original capital invested by the sole trader plus any profits which have been generated subsequently. If the sole trader has withdrawn capital (for his or her own use) the amount is shown as a deduction and is often referred to as 'drawings'.

In the case of a company with limited liability, the amount shown as equity in the balance sheet, and included in the balance sheet total, consists of the issued ordinary **share capital**. In addition, equity will include any profits which have been generated since the company was established. These profits are referred to as accumulated profits or **reserves**.

Balance sheet layout

1 You must memorise the layout of a balance sheet. If you are asked a question on this topic then you will not normally be provided with an outline of a balance sheet. Study the example of Fred's balance sheet which is given below. Memorise the layout and practise drafting a balance sheet on a blank sheet of paper.

2 Carefully note the headings of a balance sheet. Balance sheets are always labelled 'as at' a certain date.

3 Layout is important. Note the 'columns' that the figures are contained in. Structuring a balance sheet in this manner will help you fully answer the question by including all the relevant items.

4 You must clearly show fixed assets. You should specifically ensure that you give a title and date the balance sheet with a formal heading such as 'Balance sheet as at 31 December 2007'. Remember to show fixed assets and the deduction for accumulated depreciation which results in the figure for net book value. The depreciation column is the total amount of depreciation that has been charged since the fixed assets were acquired.

5 Do not forget to deduct the *total* provision for bad and doubtful debts from the figure for debtors in the balance sheet. The *total* provision is the provision for bad and doubtful debts as stated in the trial balance which is then amended by the increase or decrease in the provision. If you are uncertain about how this should be done, read section 5 again on 'bad and doubtful debts'.

6 Always show any prepayments (amounts paid in advance – see the notes at the end of the trial balance) under current assets; and show any accruals (amounts unpaid or outstanding) in current liabilities.

7 In the case of a sole trader, add the profit back to capital and *deduct* drawings.

8 Sometimes you may be given the trial balance of a limited company. In which case you will note the appearance of **share capital** and **dividends**. A limited company will normally show ordinary share capital and, in addition, you will occasionally find preference shares. A company will frequently pay a dividend based on both these types of share capital.

9 You should carefully check the trial balance and the supporting notes at the bottom of the trial balance to gather information on the dividends. For example, the notes might indicate that the company has issued ordinary share capital of £10,000 and proposes to pay a final dividend of 5 per cent. You must calculate the 5 per cent dividend on the amount of **issued share capital** and not profits. A common mistake in exams is that some students calculate the dividend as 5 per cent of the **net profits** of the company. This is wrong. You must find 5 per cent of £10,000. The same principles apply to preference shares. Additionally be careful about distinguishing between the types of dividends. Many companies pay an interim dividend (a dividend paid part way through the year) – and then another dividend – the final dividend – at the end of the year. If an interim dividend has been paid, it will be shown as an entry in the trial balance but the final dividend is not paid until just after the year-end. Therefore, in many companies the proposed final dividend that has been recommended by the directors will be outstanding at the year-end. Both the interim (paid) dividend *and* the final (proposed) dividend are shown (after the net profit) in the trading and profit and loss account. However, you should show *only* the outstanding (final) dividend as a current liability in the balance sheet. Note that there is an important difference between international accounting standards and UK financial reporting standards. International accounting standards do not recognise proposed dividends as a current liability at the financial year end. In contrast, UK financial reporting standards do recognise proposed dividends as a liability at the financial year end. What we have described in this paragraph is the UK position, not the position accepted by international accounting standards.

10 Additionally, you might sometimes notice that the examiner has supplied you with two figures for, say, ordinary share capital. For example, in the trial balance there might be reference to 'issued share capital', which has a £1,000 credit balance. In the notes, it might also be stated that the **authorised share capital** is £1,500. There is an important difference between the authorised and

issued capital. The authorised capital is the maximum share capital that the company is authorised to issue, whereas the issued share capital is the amount of shares that have actually been issued to shareholders. Remember to show **only** the issued share capital in the balance sheet.

Example layout of a balance sheet of a sole trader

(Figures have been entered so that you can understand the layout better.)

Fred's Business: balance sheet as at 31 December 2007

	£ Cost	£ Acc depn	£ Net book value
Fixed assets			
Plant and machinery	20,000	5,000	15,000
Motor vehicles	15,000	2,000	13,000
	35,000	7,000	28,000
Current assets			
Stock		5,000	
Debtors	4,000		
Less: provision			
for doubtful debts	500	3,500	
Prepaid expenses		250	
Cash in hand		500	
		9,250	
Current liabilities			
Trade creditors	6,000		
Accrued expenses	250	6,250	
Net current assets			3,000
			31,000
Long term liability			
Bank loan			12,000
Net assets			19,000
Represented by:			
Capital account			12,500
Add: profit	8,500		
Less: drawings	2,000		6,500
			19,000

Textbook guide

ATRILL AND MCLANEY: *Chapter 2*
BRITTON AND WATERSTON: *Chapter 2*
HAND, ISAAKS AND SANDERSON: *Chapter 5*
JONES: *Chapter 5*

8	
the profit and loss account	

All types of business need to prepare a profit and loss account (sometimes called an income statement) at least once a year. The profit and loss account provides a statement of a company's financial performance during the course of its last financial year. Essentially, the profit and loss account of a business records the sales (revenue) and expenses to determine whether a profit (i.e. sales exceeding expenses) or loss (i.e. expenses exceeding sales) has occurred.

Preparation of a profit and loss account

Once a business has prepared a trial balance, the next stage is to move to the construction of a profit and loss account.

In examination questions, you will not normally be provided with the layout of a profit and loss account. You will be expected to remember the complete layout. Study the layout below and commit it to memory.

As you study the layout of the profit and loss account below carefully note the following:

1 Always show the name of the individual or business for which you are preparing the final accounts.

2 Always write the heading for the profit and loss account and always provide a date. For example, below, the profit and loss account is being prepared for the whole 12 months to the 31 December 2007.

3 Give particular attention to the columns that contain the narrative and the figures. Figures are provided so that you can see how the use of columns can improve clarity and it will allow the examiner to understand what you are doing.

Once you start preparing the final accounts it is a good idea to tick off each item in the trial balance each time you take an entry from the trial balance and put it into the trading and profit and loss account or balance sheet.

Example layout of a trading and profit and loss account of a sole trader

Fred's Business: profit and loss account for the year ended 31 December 2007

	£	£
Sales		77,000
Less: cost of goods sold		
Opening stock	4,000	
Add: purchases	24,000	
Add: carriage inwards	2,000	
	30,000	
Less: closing stock	5,000	25,000
Gross profit		52,000
Add: rent received		2,000
Discount received		3,000
		57,000
Less: expenses		
Salaries and wages	20,000	
Carriage outwards	1,600	
Discount allowed	1,000	
Rent and cleaning	3,400	
Machinery repairs	500	
Advertising	1,500	
Telecommunications	2,000	

Vehicle expenses	2,500	
Electricity	3,000	
Stationery	1,000	
Bad debts	3,500	
Increase in provision		
for doubtful debts	5,000	
Depreciation:		
Plant and machinery	1,500	
Motor vehicles	2,000	48,500
Net profit		8,500

4 Now obtain a blank sheet of paper and write down the layout of a profit and loss account with your own figures – *without* looking at the above layout.

5 Sometimes in examinations you may be given different expenses from those listed above. If so, just include these expenses in the profit and loss account.

6 Only put expenses in the profit and loss account and *never* include the cost of buying an asset such as a building or machine that you intend to use in the business for many years. (The cost of buying an asset goes in the balance sheet – see previous section.)

7 Specific points in the trading and profit and loss account:

   (a) Carriage inwards is an expense of transporting or delivering goods into the business. It is accounted as an addition to the purchase cost. So simply add carriage in (or inwards) back to the purchase figure. Carriage out (or outwards) is the cost of delivering your sales to your customers. Carriage out is treated just like any other expense (such as rent, heating or lighting).

   (b) Do not forget to *add* **opening stock** to purchases and then *deduct* closing stock from the total. The opening stock figure is normally shown in the trial balance with the closing stock figure shown as a note at the bottom of the trial balance.

   (c) Do not forget to adjust for accruals and prepayments. If the notes to a trial balance state that some expenses are still outstanding (i.e. unpaid) you must add them back and include them in the expense figure in the profit and loss account. Likewise if any expenses (e.g. rent or insurance) are shown in the notes as being paid in advance, then these prepayments must be deducted from the expense that is shown in the trial balance. (Please read section 3 on accruals and prepayments.)

(d) Discounts allowed are discounts that a business has given to its customers – and are shown as an expense. However, businesses may also receive a discount (termed discounts received) in which case discounts received are *added* back to gross profit.

(e) Remember to include only the increase or decrease in the provision for doubtful debts. Ensure you understand the difference between 'bad debts written off' and 'provision for doubtful debts'. 'Bad debts written off' are shown in their entirety in the profit and loss account but you must show only the change in the provision for doubtful debts in the profit and loss account (see section 5).

(f) In most trial balances you will find an entry relating to depreciation of a fixed asset. Read the notes carefully at the bottom of a trial balance and study the depreciation method you are required to use in calculating the depreciation charge as an expense in the profit and loss account. (Please read section 6 on fixed assets and depreciation.) You should regard depreciation as a major topic since it is frequently examined.

(g) If you are preparing the final accounts of a limited company you should have dividends appearing as an appropriation of profits after the net profit has been determined. For example if a company's net profit is £10,000 then the dividends are deducted from this £10,000 figure. However, if you are preparing the final accounts for a non-limited company, such as a sole trader, then 'drawings' will effectively replace dividends.

Textbook guide

ATRILL AND MCLANEY: *Chapter 2*
BRITTON AND WATERSTON: *Chapter 3*
HAND, ISAAKS AND SANDERSON: *Chapter 5*
JONES: *Chapter 4*

9

the cash flow statement

Background

The **cash flow statement** is a relative newcomer to financial reporting. In the UK, until 1991, cash flow statements were published on a voluntary basis. Then in 1991 the UK **Accounting Standards Board** published FRS 1, *Cash Flow Statements*. Since 2005 quoted companies in the UK and the European Union have been following IAS 7, *Cash Flow Statements*, published by the International Accounting Standards Board. At one time there was a debate over whether the profit and loss account was superior to the cash flow statement or vice versa, but now it seems to be widely accepted that both statements have a useful (and complementary) role to play in reporting business financial performance.

Rationale

In order to understand the rationale for cash flow statements in company reporting, it is important to appreciate what the cash flow statement is trying to achieve and how it is different from the profit and loss account. IAS 7 states that 'information about the cash flows of an entity is useful in providing users of financial statements with a basis to assess the ability of the entity to generate cash and cash equivalents and the needs of the entity to utilise those cash flows.' This highlights a crucial difference between the profit and loss account and the cash flow statement. The purpose of the cash flow statement is to show how the business has generated cash (for instance by trading and raising finance) and how it has used those cash flows (for instance to purchase fixed assets or pay dividends to shareholders). Remember that the profit and loss account provides limited information about fixed assets (only to show how they are depreciating over time). Also the profit and loss account does not provide information about how the company has increased sources of finance (such as ordinary shares and loans).

There are a number of arguments which have been put forward in favour of cash flow reporting. One of the strongest arguments is that cash is such an important factor in determining a firm's prospects for survival that cash flow information is essential. Firms can fail, not through a lack of 'accounting profits' but from a shortage of cash. Historic cost accounting can often give an over-optimistic view of a firm's performance, especially during a period of rising prices. So cash flow reporting might make a company more cautious, for instance with respect to its dividend distribution policy. For example, a firm whose profits are largely represented by increases in stocks and debtors might want to think seriously about paying a large dividend. A large dividend payment to shareholders might have to be financed by increasing its **overdraft**, which might not be a prudent decision.

Another argument in favour of cash flow reporting is that the allocation of revenues and expenses to distinct time periods is avoided. Cash flow accounting does not involve the subjective assumptions which are associated with the profit and loss account and its reliance on accruals accounting conventions. In that sense, cash flow accounting is more objective. Cash flow reports cannot be distorted by certain types of accounting manipulation (for instance, changing the depreciation policy, or changing the basis on which provisions for doubtful debts are calculated). Moreover, cash flow statements are simpler and should be easier to understand, especially by readers of accounts who do not have a strong background in accounting.

It is true that cash flow accounting avoids time period allocation. On the other hand, it is left to the reader to interpret the information contained in a cash flow statement. Consider the case of a firm which changes the credit terms of its customers in a particular year, so that they are required to settle their debts earlier than before. A profit and loss account would show no increase in sales revenue. But a cash flow statement would show an increase in cash received from customers, which is of course a benefit in terms of improved **liquidity**, but this could just be a 'one-off' benefit that could not be repeated in future years. So a cash flow statement could give the misleading impression that the business had benefited from a 'permanent' improvement in its financial performance.

Approaches

The different approaches of the cash flow statement and the profit and loss account can be illustrated by considering how a business reports on the cash it receives from its customers. In the profit and loss account, the calculation of a provision for doubtful debts will depend upon the view taken by the firm's accountants of the likelihood that certain debtors may eventually turn out to be bad. Even though the information is 'estimated' it is likely to be useful to readers of accounts. Thus accruals based accounting systems incorporate estimates of future events into their data. On the other hand, a straightforward cash flow report would avoid such estimates, since it would report only on the actual cash received from the firm's customers.

> Make sure you understand the difference between a **cash flow statement** and a cash forecast. A cash flow statement is a historic financial report which gives information about cash flows in the past. This is the statement published by companies in their annual accounts. A cash forecast, on the other hand, is an internal report prepared by a firm's management accountants which attempts to forecast the future cash inflows and outflows for some months or years into the future.

Cash flow statements can be prepared in two distinct formats known as the *direct method* and the *indirect method*.

Direct method

Under the direct method, a cash flow statement typically presents the following information:

Cash flow statement for the year ended 31 December 2007 (direct method)

	£000	£000
Cash flows from operating activities		
Cash receipts from customers	900	
Cash paid to suppliers and employees	(520)	
Net cash from operating activities		380
Returns on investment and servicing of finance		
Interest received	30	
Interest paid	(50)	(20)
Taxation		(75)

Capital expenditure

Purchase of fixed assets	(220)	
Receipts from sales of fixed assets	19	(201)

Equity dividends paid (33)

Financing

Issue of ordinary shares	140	
Repayment of loan	(60)	80
Increase in cash		131

The direct method is so-called because it takes the relevant cash flows directly from the firm's records and enters them in the cash flow statement. (Note that cash inflows are shown as positive numbers while cash outflows are shown in brackets.)

The statement begins with the net cash inflow from the firm's operating activities, consisting of cash received from customers and cash paid to suppliers and employees. Next is shown returns on investment and servicing of finance, for example interest received from investments less interest paid on loans. The amount of taxes paid in cash is shown next under the heading 'taxation'. Capital expenditure consists of cash paid for purchase of fixed assets less any cash received from fixed assets sold during the year. Next is shown the amount of dividends paid to ordinary shareholders. The final category relates to long term finance and details issues or repurchases of ordinary share capital as well as cash received from new loans or cash paid to redeem existing loans. The total at the bottom of the statement explains the increase (or decrease) in cash between the beginning and the end of the financial year.

Indirect method

Cash flow statements can also be presented using the indirect method. This method is so-called because the information on cash flow from operating activities is derived *indirectly* from the profit and loss account.

In order to understand the rationale for the indirect method we need to remind ourselves of the main difference between a profit and loss account and a cash flow statement. The figures in a profit and loss account are prepared after the financial accountants have made a number of accruals adjustments. There are a number of accruals adjustments but the main ones are related to depreciation, stock, debtors and creditors. Try to think of it in this way. When the financial accountants prepared the profit and loss account, they took the raw data available (i.e. cash based data) and converted it into accruals based data. So, if we want to derive the figure for *cash from operating activities* (in the cash flow statement) from the operating **profit** (in the profit and loss account) we need to *reverse* the accruals adjustments which went into preparing the profit and loss account. In other words, we have to undo all the hard work of the financial accountants!

It is not surprising then that cash flow statements prepared under the indirect method are sometimes confusing to readers of accounts who have little accounting expertise. They see a statement which begins with the line operating profit. Next they see depreciation *added* to that figure to arrive at net cash from operating activities. However, if we remind ourselves that depreciation is not a cash item, then we can understand that adding back depreciation will help us to get back to the original cash data of the business.

Let us assume that during the year ended 31 December 2007 a firm charged depreciation in its profit and loss account, and, between the beginning of the year and the end of the year, stocks increased, as did debtors and creditors.

If we reverse these four accruals adjustments (relating to depreciation, stock, debtors and creditors) what do we need to do?

Depreciation

The effect of the depreciation charge in the profit and loss account is to *reduce* profit. In order to *reverse* this adjustment we need to *add back* **depreciation** to the operating profit figure.

Stock

Consider the relationship between opening stock, purchases and closing stock in the profit and loss account:

opening stock + purchases − closing stock = cost of sales

If closing stock is greater than opening stock (that is, stocks increased during the year), cost of sales will be lower and accounting profits will be higher. In order to reverse this adjustment we need to *deduct* from profit any *increase* in stock. From a perspective of working capital, an increase in stock represents an increase in (cash) resources tied up in **working capital**.

Debtors

Consider the relationship between opening debtors, sales to customers, cash received from customers, and closing debtors:

$$\text{opening debtors} + \text{sales} = \text{cash received from customers} + \text{closing debtors}$$

If the figure for closing debtors is greater than the figure for opening debtors, (that is, debtors increased during the year), cash received from customers will be lower than sales. In order to reverse this accruals adjustment we need to *deduct* from profit any *increase* in debtors. From a perspective of working capital, an increase in debtors also represents an increase in (cash) resources tied up in working capital.

Creditors

The adjustment for creditors goes in the *opposite direction* to the adjustment for debtors. Consider the relationship between opening creditors, purchases from suppliers, cash paid to suppliers, and closing creditors:

$$\text{opening creditors} + \text{purchases} = \text{cash paid to suppliers} + \text{closing creditors}$$

If the figure for closing creditors is greater than the figure for opening creditors, (that is, creditors increased during the year), cash paid to suppliers will be lower than purchases. In order to reverse this accruals adjustment we need to *add to* profit any *increase* in creditors. From a perspective of working capital, an increase in creditors represents a decrease in (cash) resources tied up in working capital.

Stock, debtors and creditors form a major part of working capital and these three accruals adjustments are often referred to as working capital adjustments. The effect of these three accruals adjustments can be summarised as follows:

Change in balance sheet item over one year	Required adjustment to convert operating profit to cash inflow from operating activities
Increase in stock	decrease
Decrease in stock	increase

Increase in debtors	decrease
Decrease in debtors	increase
Increase in creditors	increase
Decrease in creditors	decrease

EXAMPLE QUESTION

Cash flow statement using indirect method

You are given the following information concerning a company whose financial year end is 31 December 2007:

	31 Dec 2006	31 Dec 2007
	£000	£000
Stock	700	790
Debtors	460	440
Creditors	620	650

You are also told that the depreciation charge in the accounts for the year ended 31 December 2007 amounted to £295,000 and that profit before taxation amounted to £125,000.

Required

Prepare a cash flow statement, using the indirect method and also making use of the information contained in the cash flow statement above based on the direct method.

Suggested answer

Cash flow statement for the year ended 31 December 2007 (indirect method)

	£000	£000
Cash flows from operating activities		
Operating profit		125
Adjustments for:		
Depreciation		295
Stock		(90)
Debtors		20

Creditors		30
Net cash from operating activities		380
Returns on investment		
and servicing of finance		
Interest received	30	
Interest paid	(50)	(20)
Taxation		(75)
Capital expenditure		
Purchase of fixed assets	(220)	
Receipts from sales of fixed assets	19	(201)
Equity dividends paid		(33)
Financing		
Issue of ordinary shares	140	
Repayment of loan	(60)	80
Increase in cash		131

Depreciation is an accruals figure and does not represent a movement in cash flows. Therefore, we need to *add back* to profit before taxation the depreciation charge of £295,000 to arrive at a cash flow figure.

The increase in stock represents an increase in working capital and we therefore need to *decrease* profit before tax. The decrease amounts to £90,000.

The decrease in debtors represents a decrease in working capital and we therefore need to *increase* profit before tax. The increase amounts to £20,000.

The increase in creditors represents a decrease in working capital and we therefore need to *increase* profit before tax. The increase amounts to £30,000.

> Note that the top section of the cash flow statement (indirect method) is effectively a reconciliation between the figure for profit before taxation (taken from the profit and loss account) and the figure for net cash from operating activities.

ATRILL AND MCLANEY: *Chapter 5*
BRITTON AND WATERSTON: *Chapter 9*
HAND, ISAAKS AND SANDERSON: *Chapter 7*
JONES: *Chapter 8*

10

preparing the final accounts (worked example)

You are now in a position to prepare a profit and loss account and balance sheet as might be required in a typical exam question.

Work through *every* entry paying careful attention to the layout of the profit and loss account and balance sheet.

In this question, you are dealing with a public limited company (Plc) rather than a sole trader. Therefore, you should expect to find entries in the trial balance for share capital and dividends. Remember to put both the interim and final dividends at the bottom of the trading and profit and loss account and put the share capital and outstanding (unpaid) dividends in the balance sheet.

Worked example: Tasty Cakes Plc

Tasty Cakes Plc is a company that makes and sells a range of high quality cakes to retail outlets. The company was formed with an authorised share capital of 100,000 ordinary shares of £1 each and 30,000 10 per cent preference shares of £1 each.

At 31 December 2007, the company accountant extracted the following trial balance from the company's records:

	£	£
Issued ordinary share capital		80,000
Issued 10% preference share capital		8,000
Cake machinery (at cost)	30,000	
Delivery vehicles (at cost)	22,000	
Debtors and creditors	32,250	16,550
Cash	63,200	
12% debentures		10,000
Stock (1 January 2007)	22,350	
Sundry expenses	10,800	
Purchases and sales	132,250	198,575
Bad debts written off	2,250	
Salaries and wages of employees	24,575	
Insurance of delivery vehicles	550	
Provision for depreciation:		
Cake machinery		14,000
Delivery vehicles		8,000
Interim preference dividend paid	400	
Profit and loss account		
(1 January 2007)		5,500
Provision for doubtful		
debts (1 January 2007)		600
Debenture interest	600	
	341,225	341,225

You are also provided with the following additional information:

(a) Stock at 31 December 2007 is valued at £24,250.

(b) Depreciation on machinery is to be provided for at the rate of 10 per cent per annum using the straight line basis.

(c) Depreciation on delivery vehicles is to be provided for at the rate of 20 per cent per annum using the reducing balance method.

(d) Insurance prepaid at 31 December 2007 amounted to £200.

(e) Sundry expenses owing at 31 December 2007 amounted to £400.

(f) The provision for doubtful debts is to be increased to £900.

(g) The directors propose to pay an ordinary dividend of 5 per cent to the ordinary shareholders and to pay the remaining dividend due to the preference shareholders.

(h) Corporation tax of £5,000 is to be provided for.

(i) £3,000 is to be transferred to general reserve.

Required

Prepare the profit and loss account for the year ended 31 December 2007 and a balance sheet as at that date.

Suggested answer

Tasty Cakes Plc: profit and loss account for the year ended 31 December 2007

	£	£
Sales		198,575
Less: cost of goods sold		
Opening stock	22,350	
Add: purchases	132,250	
	154,600	
Less: closing stock	24,250	130,350
Gross profit		68,225
Less: expenses		
Miscellaneous expenses (10,800 + 400)	11,200	
Bad debts	2,250	
Increase in provision for doubtful debts	300	
Salaries and wages	24,575	
Insurance (550 – 200)	350	
Debenture interest (600 + 600)	1,200	
Depreciation: cake machinery	3,000	
Depreciation: delivery vehicles	2,800	45,675
Net profit before tax		22,550
Less: tax		5,000
		17,550
Less: proposed ordinary share dividends	4,000	
preference dividend	800	4,800
		12,750
Transfer to general reserve		3,000
Net profit		9,750

Notes

Depreciation of cake machinery = 10% x £30,000 = £3,000.
Depreciation of delivery vehicles = 20% x (£22,000 – £8,000) = £2,800
Debenture interest: the trial balance shows that £600 was paid during the year, therefore £600 is outstanding at the year end, making a total charge of £1,200.
Preference dividend: the trial balance shows that £400 was paid during the year, therefore £400 is outstanding at the year end, making a total charge of £800.

Tasty Cakes Plc Balance sheet as at 31 December 2007

	£ Cost	£ Acc depn	£ Net book value
Fixed assets			
Cake machinery	30,000	17,000	13,000
Delivery vehicles	22,000	10,800	11,200
	52,000	27,800	24,200
Current assets			
Stock	24,250		
Debtors (32,250 – 900)	31,350		
Insurance prepayment	200		
Cash	63,200	119,000	
Current liabilities			
Creditors	16,550		
Accrued expenses	400		
Preference dividends	400		
Ordinary share dividends	4,000		
Debenture interest	600		
Tax	5,000	26,950	
Net current assets			92,050
			116,250
Long term liability			
12% Debentures			10,000
Net assets			106,250

Share capital		
Ordinary shares		80,000
Preference shares		8,000
Reserves		
General reserve		3,000
Opening profit	5,500	
Retained profit for the year	9,750	15,250
		106,250

11

analysis of company financial statements

Once a business has produced its financial statements an important next step is to interpret the information that has been provided. This interpretation can help the owner, partners or shareholders to evaluate the information contained in the financial statements to draw inferences and conclusions.

A key analytical tool in examining accounts is the use of ratio analysis. Ratios are concerned with the relationship between key figures in financial statements. Ratios can be used to establish and compare a trend of figures within the same business or to compare similar sized businesses in the same sector with each other.

Although there are no definitive categories of ratios, it is often convenient to classify ratios under the following key headings:

- profitability
- liquidity
- efficiency
- financial

Profitability

Profitability can be defined as the ability of a business or company to generate profits.

Return on capital employed (ROCE)

A major profitability ratio is the **return on capital employed** (often abbreviated to **ROCE**). This ratio highlights the reported profit in relation to the investment in the business. (The investment in the business is often defined as fixed assets plus current assets less current liabilities.) Sometimes gross capital is employed which is fixed assets plus current assets. However, there are many ways to define profit. It is possible to use the net profit, gross profit, profit before interest and tax, operating profit etc.

$$\text{ROCE (\%)} = \frac{\text{Net profit}}{\text{Net capital employed}} \times 100$$

(Do note that this 'ratio' is normally expressed as a percentage.)

For example, if a business obtains a net profit (i.e. a return) of £150 and has **net capital employed** of £1,000 then the business obtains a 15 per cent return on the capital invested in the business. In other words, for every £1 invested in the business, investors obtain 15p return on their invested funds. An investor can then decide if the risk involved in this business is worth the 15 per cent return compared, perhaps, with other business opportunities.

Sales margin

Profitability can also be assessed by comparing profits to sales revenue to highlight the profit that is obtained from sales to customers. This ratio is often called a sales margin ratio.

It is possible to find the profit margins by using net profit (that is, profit available for shareholders) or operating profit or gross profit.

If the net profit is £250 and the sales are £2,500, then:

net profit : sales is

£250 : £2,500 = 10%

(Note this ratio is normally expressed as a percentage.)

This 10 per cent figure means that for every £1 of goods that are sold to customers the business receives a 10p net profit. This 10p figure can then be compared with previous years or with sales margins in other businesses.

Asset turnover

The asset turnover ratio determines the amount of sales that are generated from the capital invested in the business. The ratio is calculated as:

$$\text{sales : net capital employed}$$

(Note that sometimes gross capital employed is used.)

If sales are £2,500 and net capital employed is £1,000 then the resulting ratio of 2.5 : 1 means that for every £1 invested in the business, £2.5 of sales are generated. The ratio indicates how intensively a business is using its assets to generate sales.

Liquidity

Although a business must at least be profitable in the longer term, it is vital that in the short term it has sufficient funds to meet its day-to-day expenses and obligations. From a business perspective, liquidity can be viewed as having the cash funds necessary to meet debts and obligations as and when they fall due for payment. In practice, for example, liquidity means that a company has sufficient funds to pay its suppliers, employees and be able to meet its interest obligations to banks.

The importance of liquidity can be evidenced in a company's cash cycle. A company will receive cash largely from debtors and cash sales. At the same time cash is being recycled and paid out to creditors, suppliers, employees (for salaries and wages) and for other expenses.

The company must keep its cash inflows and cash outflows under close control. If its cash cycle becomes unbalanced or distorted then a business may find that its cash inflows are insufficient to meet its cash outflows. The result can then mean liquidity problems for the business.

Many businesses often find maintaining a liquid position difficult. For example, many debtors do not pay their debts on time – whilst many creditors frequently demand early payments from businesses.

Also, in the context of liquidity, stock levels have to be monitored carefully. Many companies often tie up a large amount of their resources in stock. At times, these stock levels can be too high because excessive levels of stock are maintained. These large amounts of stock have to be financed, often by overdraft or loan. In addition, the stock is exposed to the possibility of damage, obsolescence and theft. By carefully monitoring levels of demand and the lead-time (the time stock takes from being ordered to arriving in the warehouse), a business should be able to minimise stock levels and reduce the liquid resources tied up in stock.

In many businesses, there is frequently a trade off between liquidity and profitability. To be as profitable as possible, a company should invest most of its available resources including liquid assets into its productive assets (such as in factories, machinery, offices, etc.) However, the danger is that if a company 'over-invests' in productive capacity then it will reduce its liquid (working capital) funds and may possibly become illiquid. On the other hand, if a company has excessively high levels of cash and other liquid resources (i.e. it is too liquid) then the company is under-utilising its resources and will be less profitable than it might be otherwise.

Current ratio

One of the most significant indicators of liquidity is the **current ratio** (or working capital ratio). It is defined as:

$$\text{current assets (CA) : current liabilities (CL)}$$

If current assets are £2,000 and current liabilities are £1,500 the resulting ratio of 1.33 : 1 (2,000 : 1,500) indicates that for every £1 of current liabilities the business has £1.33 of current assets with which to pay them.

This ratio can vary greatly between companies in differing types of business. For example, a retail shop whose customers pay predominantly in cash will be able to let its working capital ratio fall to, say, 0.3 : 1. This means that for every £1 of debts and other short-term commitments the company has £0.30 of current assets with which to meet its obligations. A low current ratio is normally acceptable in a cash based retail business because of the high velocity of cash transactions. In other words, the business will have little or no debtors and will not need to wait to receive its cash. The business will receive a cash inflow as soon as a sale is made. In contrast, other organisations such as a manufacturing company may trade with its customers predominantly on credit. Such a business may have to wait many months after a sale has been made to receive a cash payment from customers. As a result credit based businesses frequently need to have higher current assets in order to meet their current liabilities. In this type of business, a current ratio of 1.5 or 1.6 : 1 is not unusual.

Quick asset (or acid test) ratio

Another liquidity ratio is termed the quick asset or **acid test ratio**. Quick assets are defined as current assets but excluding stock (in other words, debtors plus cash).

In many businesses, stock can take a considerable length of time to convert into cash. So the current or working capital ratio is modified in order to focus on quick assets. The quick assets are then compared with current liabilities.

The quick assets (QA) ratio is defined as:

$$(CA - stock) : current\ liabilities\ (CL)$$

So, if the current assets of a business are £2,000 and stock is £250, the quick assets are £1,750.

If current liabilities are £1,500, then the quick asset ratio is:

$$QA : CL$$

$$(2,000 - 250) : 1,500$$

$$1,750 : 1,500 = 1.17 : 1$$

This ratio means that for every £1 of current liabilities the business has £1.17 of quick assets in which to pay its commitments. Normally businesses nowadays expect this ratio not to fall much below the 1 : 1 level, although businesses whose sales are largely cash based can permit this ratio to fall to as low as 0.2 : 1.

Efficiency ratios

The internal efficiency of the operations of a business is important. Efficiency ratios primarily examine how productively companies utilise and manage their stock, debtors, creditors and other business aspects.

Efficiency ratios can be calculated for most types of financial information relating to a business. But it is important to remember that whatever efficiency ratios are calculated – they must be relevant and meaningful.

Stock turnover

The **stock turnover** ratio is important in measuring the length of time that a business has, on average, stock in its warehouse. In calculating this ratio it is normal practice to use the cost price of sales (rather than selling price) since stocks are themselves shown at cost price.

This ratio can be expressed either in terms of a turnover rate or in days (or months).

$$\text{stock turnover (rate)} = \frac{\text{cost of sales}}{\text{average stocks}}$$

Average stocks are normally taken to be a simple average of opening and closing stocks, that is:

$$\frac{\text{opening stocks} + \text{closing stocks}}{2}$$

Alternatively stock turnover can be calculated as a number of days (or months).

Thus:

$$\text{stock turnover (days)} = \frac{\text{average stocks}}{\text{cost of sales}} \times 365 \text{ days}$$

For example, if average stock levels are £1,000 and cost of sales are £4,000 then the stock turnover (in days) is:

$$\frac{1,000}{4,000} \times 365 = 91.25 \text{ days.}$$

In other words, the business has 91.25 days worth of sales in the warehouse. However, this ratio must be analysed carefully because it can vary considerably between different types of business. For example, a business trading in highly perishable food might aim to hold no stock at the end of each day (i.e. its stock turnover ratio is just 1 day). In contrast, a business trading in non-perishable goods may need to maintain high stock levels for customer choice. It could also be the case that the business has to cope with a long or erratic lead-time in obtaining new supplies. In such cases the stock turnover ratio could be many months.

By carefully monitoring this ratio a business should be able to ensure that it does not carry too much or too little stock.

Debtors' collection (or turnover)

Most companies conduct their business based on credit. Goods are sold to customers on credit and at a future date the customer is expected to pay for these goods. Effectively, the business is providing finance to the debtor from the time of sale to the time at which payment is received. The debtors' collection ratio can calculate the average number of days that debtors take in paying for their goods. An excessively lengthy period in waiting for a debtor to pay a business invoice can result in substantial funds being unnecessarily tied up in debtors.

The debtors collection ratio is:

$$\text{debtor collection period (days)} = \frac{\text{average debtors}}{\text{credit sales}} \times 365$$

For example, if the average debtors are £500 and the credit sales are £2,500, the debtors' collection period is:

$$\frac{500}{2,500} \times 365 = 73 \text{ days}$$

That is, on average, it takes 73 days for debtors to pay their invoices.

Note that in some businesses, such as in the cash retail trade – whose customers pay predominantly in cash – this ratio has limited value.

Creditors' payment

In a similar manner to the previous ratio, it is possible to calculate the average time that it takes a business to pay its creditors by calculating the creditors' payment period. Effectively the business is receiving finance from the creditor from the time of purchase to the time at which payment is made.

The ratio is:

$$\text{creditors' payment period (days)} = \frac{\text{average creditors}}{\text{credit purchases}} \times 365$$

In both the above formulae, the average debtors and average creditors can be found as a simple average, that is:

$$\frac{\text{opening balance} + \text{closing balance}}{2}$$

Financial ratios

Gearing (leverage)

Gearing (or sometimes referred to as leverage) identifies the extent to which a business is financed by outside sources of debt.

In particular, gearing compares the amount of long term loans and debentures (indebtedness) with shareholders' funds (i.e. the ordinary share capital plus reserves). For simplicity, long term loans and debentures are usually referred to as 'debt' while **shareholders' funds** are referred to as 'equity'. The gearing ratio examines the relationship between debt and equity.

A business that is financed by a higher proportion of debt is deemed to be more highly geared than a company that is financed predominantly by the shareholders' equity.

The two major sources of financing for a business are through equity and debt. Since gearing is the relationship between these two funding sources it can have an important effect on the long term financial stability of a business.

The importance of gearing is that interest on loans and debentures must normally be paid whatever the level of profitability. On the other hand, the level of dividends paid to shareholders is determined annually by the board of directors. In times of reduced profitability, a company can reduce its dividends but will be unable to reduce its interest on debentures and loans.

So, in times of adversity with falling profitability, the interest payments must still be made but there is no similar obligation to pay dividends to shareholders. In such circumstances, a relatively low-geared company will be in a stronger position to survive by being able to cut its relatively larger proportion of (optional) dividends.

However, in times of prosperity, a higher geared company can achieve superior returns. Once the interest has been paid there are often proportionately more profits to be made available to shareholders as dividends.

There are several definitions of gearing.

$$\text{gearing (\%)} = \frac{\text{debt}}{\text{debt} + \text{equity}}$$

Where: debt = long term loans and debentures
equity = shareholders' funds

An alternative (and more simplistic) definition is:

$$\text{gearing (\%)} = \frac{\text{debt}}{\text{equity}}$$

Sometimes, because preference shares have some similar characteristics to loan capital, the definition of debt can be amended to include preference shares.

Dividend yield

The dividend yield ratio explains the gross dividend that an investor will receive in relation to the market price of the share:

$$\text{dividend yield (\%)} = \frac{\text{gross dividend}}{\text{market price of ordinary share}}$$

Note that, in the UK, companies pay dividends net of lower rate income tax. Provided the net dividend (after deduction of tax) is known, then the gross dividend (before deduction of tax) can be calculated. For instance, let us assume that the UK lower rate of income tax is 10 per cent and the net dividend is 18p. The gross dividend (g) can be calculated as:

$$g \times (1 - 0.1) = 18p$$

$$g = \frac{18p}{0.9} = 20p$$

So, if the gross dividend is 20p and the market share price is 200p the dividend yield is:

$$\frac{20p}{200p} \times 100 = 10\%$$

Investors seeking a higher income will select a company with a high dividend yield – whilst investors requiring greater capital growth in their investment in equities might consider selecting a company with a lower yield.

Interest cover

This ratio is important in providing an indication of the extent to which profits can fall before the payment of interest is placed at risk. It is usually defined as:

$$\text{interest cover (times)} = \frac{\text{profit before interest and tax}}{\text{interest payable}}$$

So, if profit before interest and tax is £1,000 and interest payable is £250, the interest cover is 4 times. In other words the business can pay its interest 4 times from the current level of profits. There is no hard and fast rule, but it is often thought that the higher the ratio the greater the degree of interest cover safeguard (or safety margin) there is for the business.

Dividend cover

The dividend cover ratio examines the extent to which profits could fall before the payment of dividends is placed at risk.

$$\text{Dividend cover ratio (times)} = \frac{\text{profit available for ordinary shareholders}}{\text{ordinary dividends paid}}$$

If a company has £500 net profits and currently pays £125 in ordinary dividends, the dividend cover ratio is £500/£125 = 4 times.

This ratio means that profits can fall to one quarter of their current level before the current dividend is placed at risk.

Benefits of financial ratio analysis

The analysis of financial statements may be useful in:

- providing advice on buying and selling of shares;
- deciding whether to lend money to a company;
- ascertaining the value of a company in takeover situations;
- helping to determine the value of a company for taxation purposes.

In your overall analysis of a business, in addition to the financial information from the financial statements, you may also need to ascertain other factors such as:

- the company's history;
- the structure of the company;
- details of the experience and qualifications of directors/management;
- the products of the business and type and nature of its markets;
- details of competitors;
- the nature of the industry in which the company operates.

Limitations of financial ratios

Financial ratio analysis can be very useful in suggesting ways to improve a company's performance. However, it needs to be remembered that performance evaluation based on financial ratios needs to be conducted with some care. Ratios by themselves rarely offer conclusive proof about managerial performance.

For example, a firm might appear to be performing poorly compared with the previous year. But if the entire industry is experiencing economic problems (for instance, a building industry recession), then, relative to the rest of the industry, that particular firm may be doing quite well. Companies in different industries may have different trading patterns. For instance, a supermarket chain may have a low level of debtors relative to sales, which is typical for that particular industry. So a comparison with an engineering firm which might have a much higher level of debtors would need to take this industry difference into account. Sometimes the most relevant data is simply not available. Thus the calculation of the debtors' collection ratio is based on a comparison of trade debtors and credit sales. However, if it is not possible to obtain a breakdown of sales between credit sales and cash sales then the total sales figure would have to be used, but with an acceptance that there is an inevitable degree of error in the calculation.

Nevertheless, a thoughtful approach to ratio analysis can help to build up an overall picture of performance which may help to suggest the most useful questions to ask.

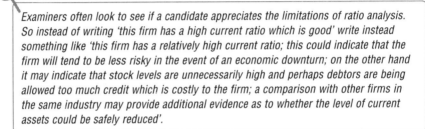

Examiners often look to see if a candidate appreciates the limitations of ratio analysis. So instead of writing 'this firm has a high current ratio which is good' write instead something like 'this firm has a relatively high current ratio; this could indicate that the firm will tend to be less risky in the event of an economic downturn; on the other hand it may indicate that stock levels are unnecessarily high and perhaps debtors are being allowed too much credit which is costly to the firm; a comparison with other firms in the same industry may provide additional evidence as to whether the level of current assets could be safely reduced'.

EXAMPLE QUESTION

Financial ratio analysis

The financial statements for two companies for the year ended 31 December 2007 contained the following information:

Oranges Ltd and Lemons Ltd. Extract from profit and loss accounts for year ended 31 December 2007

	Oranges Ltd £ 000	Lemons Ltd £ 000
Turnover	13,000	1,720
Cost of sales and other expenses	<u>8,500</u>	<u>1,570</u>
Operating profit	4,500	150

Interest		80		20
Profit before tax		4,420		130
Tax		520		64
Profit available				
for shareholders		3,900		66
Dividends		1,300		30
		2,600		36

Balance sheets as at 31 December 2007

	Oranges Ltd		Lemons Ltd	
	£000		£000	
Fixed assets				
Tangible assets	6,800		760	
Investments	160	6,960	20	780
Current assets				
Stock	700		1,100	
Debtors	420		550	
Cash	120		50	
	1,240		1,700	
Current liabilities	1,680		1,050	
Net current				
assets (liabilities)		(440)		650
Total assets less				
current liabilities		6,520		1,430
Long term liabilities		(700)		(240)
		5,820		1,190
Capital and Reserves				
Called up share capital		4,000		500
Profit and loss account		1,820		690
Shareholders' funds		5,820		1,190

Required

Calculate suitable financial ratios to compare and contrast the financial
performance of Oranges Ltd and Lemons Ltd.

Suggested solution

Key financial ratios

Profitability	Oranges Ltd	Lemons Ltd
ROCE:		
Profit available for shareholders(PAFS)/ net capital employed	3,900/6,520 = 60%	66/1,430 = 5%
Alternatively:		
ROCE: PBIT/net capital employed	4,500/6,520 = 69%	150/1,430 = 10%
Net margin: PAFS/sales	3,900/13,000 = 30%	66/1,720 = 3.8%
Gross margin: operating profit/sales	4,500/13,000 = 35%	150/1,720 = 8.7%
Total assets:		
Sales/net capital employed (Asset turnover)	13,000/6,520 = 2 times	1,720/1,430 = 1.2 times

Liquidity

Current ratio: CA/CL	1,240/1,680 = 0.74	1,700/1,050 = 1.6
Quick (acid test) ratio:	(1,240 − 700)/1,680	(1,720 − 1,100)/1,050
(CA − stock)/CL	= 0.32	= 0.59

Efficiency

Current assets: Sales/CA	13,000/1,240 = 10.5 times	1,720/1,700 = unity
Stock turnover: (stock/COS) × 365	(700/8,500) × 365 = 30 days	(1,100/1,570) × 365 = 256 days
Debtors collection: Debtors/sales × 365	(420/13,000) × 365 = 12 days	(550/1,720) × 365 = 117 days

Gearing	Oranges Ltd	Lemons Ltd
Capital: debt/(debt + equity)	700/(700 + 5,820)	240/(240 + 1,190)
	= 10.7%	= 16.8%
(where 'debt' = long term debt, and 'equity' = shareholders' funds)		
Income: interest/PBIT	80/4,500 = 1.8%	20/150 = 13.3%
Other		
Dividend cover: PAFS/ dividends	3,900/1,300 = 3 times	66/30 = 2.2 times

In the above question, the profitability ratios indicate Oranges has a return on capital employed of 69 per cent using PBIT. This means that for every £1 invested in the company, Oranges is generating 69p net profit. This ratio can then be compared with Lemons which is generating a return on capital employed of only 10 per cent. In both cases, it is necessary to make an assessment of the riskiness of the nature of businesses undertaken by these companies.

Additionally, Oranges is obtaining a much higher net profit margin on sales. The PBIT to Sales is 30 per cent in Oranges' case which means that for every £1 of goods sold to customers Oranges is obtaining 30p net profit – whereas Lemons only obtains 3.8p. To assess fully the relative profitability of these ratios, it is also important to know the type of products being sold by each of these companies because the profit margins can vary considerably between companies selling different types of products.

Oranges also has a higher asset turnover at 2 times compared with 1.2 times for Lemons. This ratio means that Oranges obtains £2 of sales from every £1 invested in the business, against £1.2 of sales in the case of Lemons.

In terms of the liquidity ratios, Lemons seems to be in a stronger position. Lemons' CA:CL ratio of 1.6 : 1 indicates that for every £1 of current liabilities, the company has £1.6 of current assets in which to pay them. Oranges' ratio is much lower at 0.74 : 1 – which means the company only has 74p to pay every £1 of current liabilities. Again, this ratio can be heavily influenced by the nature of the businesses.

If the quick assets are calculated (by excluding stock from current assets) and compared to current liabilities, then Lemons is also in a stronger position with a quick asset ratio of 0.59 : 1 compared with 0.32 : 1 for Oranges.

In terms of the efficiency ratios, the most interesting ratios concern the stock turnover and debtors' collection ratios. The stock turnover for Oranges is 30 days but it is 256 days for Lemons. This means that Lemons holds stock levels equivalent to 256 days of trading whereas Oranges at 30 days is much lower. The reasons for this difference could be because of the nature of the product, supplier difficulties or just very poor stock control.

Likewise Lemons has much a higher debtors' collection period which means that debtors take 117 days to pay for goods sold to them. In contrast, Oranges' debtors pay for their goods in a mere 12 days. This difference may be for a variety of reasons including the type of business or the nature of debtors or perhaps the level of each company's credit control.

The gearing of capital Lemons (16.8 per cent) is somewhat higher than Oranges (10.7 per cent). This means that, in relation to each company's shareholders' funds, Lemons is financed by a slightly higher proportion of debt as opposed to equity.

Gearing can also be measured as the relationship between the interest charge and profit before interest and tax. This measure of gearing is 13.3 per cent for Lemons but only 1.8 per cent for Oranges. A major factor in this case is the higher profitability of Oranges which explains the lower gearing ratio.

Finally, dividend cover works out at 3 times for oranges and 2.2 times for Lemons. In both cases there are sufficient levels of profit available to support the dividend to shareholders, although it can be noted that Oranges has relatively more resources available to reinvest in the business.

Textbook guide

ATRILL AND MCLANEY: *Chapter 6*
BRITTON AND WATERSTON: *Chapter 11*
HAND, ISAAKS AND SANDERSON: *Chapter 8*
JONES: *Chapter 9*

12

practice questions

Now put your notes away and attempt these two questions.

Bright Red Ltd involves the preparation of a balance sheet and profit and loss account.

Clear Blue Ltd requires the preparation of a cash flow statement.

Do not look at the answer until you have attempted the whole question.

PRACTICE QUESTION: Bright Red Ltd

The trial balance of Bright Red Ltd as at 31 December 2007 was as follows:

	£	£
Administration salaries	106,460	
Office expenses	11,260	
Ordinary £1 shares		300,000
Debentures 6%		100,000
Retained profits 1 January 2007		19,740
Depreciation 1 January 2007:		
Premises		23,200
Equipment		55,000
Vehicles		58,500
Premises	300,000	
Equipment	140,000	
Vehicles	170,000	
Bank		11,420
Debtors and creditors	93,600	61,560
Sales		1,205,200

	£	£
Purchases	743,400	
Opening stock	44,600	
Returns inwards	4,900	
Returns outwards		9,340
Productive wages	164,000	
Distribution expenses	65,740	
	1,843,960	1,843,960

The following information is available, none of which has been taken into account in the preparation of the trial balance above:

1 Stock as at 31 December 2007 is valued at £44,000.

2 Vehicles are primarily used for distribution; premises are used equally between production, distribution and administration; equipment is used equally between production and administration.

3 Premises are to be depreciated 1 per cent straight line, equipment 20 per cent straight line and vehicles 25 per cent reducing balance.

4 Equipment was sold on 31 December 2007 for £30,000 and this amount had been credited to sales. The original cost of the equipment was £40,000 and it had been purchased on 31 December 2004. No further entries apart from cash and sales had been made in the books of the company.

5 Bad debts of £5,200 need to be written off and a provision for doubtful debts at the rate of 5 per cent is to be introduced.

6 Taxation for the year is estimated at £19,720.

7 A final dividend of 4p per share is proposed by the directors.

8 Accruals of £7,000 for administration expenses are required and prepayments of £11,200 have been identified within distribution expenses.

9 The interest on the debentures has not yet been paid.

Required

Prepare the profit and loss account for the year ended 31 December 2007 and the balance sheet as at that date.

PRACTICE QUESTION: Clear Blue Ltd

The financial statements of Clear Blue Ltd are as follows:

Clear Blue Ltd Profit and loss accounts for the year ended 31 December

	2007	2006
	£000	£000
Profit before taxation	4,070	7,100
Corporation tax	1,500	1,900
Profit after taxation	2,570	5,200
Dividends	2,320	4,940
Retained profit/(loss) for the year	250	260

Clear Blue Ltd Balance sheet as at 31 December

	£000	2007 £000	£000	2006 £000
Fixed assets				
Cost		3,000		2,500
Accumulated depreciation		1,200		1,000
Net book value		1,800		1,500
Current assets				
Stock	4,450		3,100	
Debtors	3,700		4,000	
Cash	400		600	
	8,550		7,700	
Current liabilities				
Creditors	2,800		2,700	
Taxation payable	2,400		1,900	

Dividend payable	1,600		1,500	
	6,800		6,100	
Net current assets		1,750		1,600
		3,550		3,100
Long term liability				
Bank loan		800		600
		2,750		2,500
Represented by:				
Share capital				
Ordinary shares		2,000		2,000
Reserves				
Retained profit		750		500
		2,750		2,500

Notes

1 Profit before tax is stated after deducting:

  a interest paid of £74,000 in 2007;
  b the depreciation charge of £550,000 for 2007.

2 The original cost of fixed assets sold in 2007 was £600,000.
3 Loss on sale of fixed assets in 2007 amounted to £80,000.

Required

1 Prepare a cash flow statement (indirect method) for the year end 31 December 2007.

2 Draw up 'T' accounts for fixed assets, taxation and dividends.

Suggested answer: Bright Red Ltd

Bright Red Ltd. Profit and loss account for year ended 31 December 2007

	£	£	£
Sales (1,205,200 – 4,900 – 30,000)			1,170,300
Less: cost of goods sold			
Opening stock		44,600	
Add: purchases (743,400 – 9,340)		734,060	
		778,660	
Less closing stock		44,000	
Cost of sales			734,660
Gross profit			435,640

Production expenses:

Productive wages	164,000	
Depreciation of premises	1,000	
Depreciation of equipment	10,000	
Profit on sale of equipment	(7,000)	168,000

Administrative expenses:

Administration salaries	106,460
Office expenses	11,260
Depreciation of premises	1,000
Depreciation of equipment	10,000
Profit on sale of equipment	(7,000)
Bad debts	5,200
Doubtful debt provision (5% × (93,600 – 5,200))	4,420

Accrued expenses	<u>7,000</u>	138,340	

Distribution expenses:

Distribution expenses (65,740 – 11,200)	54,540		
Depreciation of premises	1,000		
Depreciation of vehicles	<u>27,875</u>	<u>83,415</u>	<u>389,755</u>
Profit before interest and tax			45,885
Debenture interest (6% × 100,000)			<u>6,000</u>
Profit after interest before tax			39,885
Taxation			<u>19,720</u>
Profit after interest and tax			20,165
Ordinary dividend (4% × 300,000)			<u>12,000</u>
Retained profit for year			<u>8,165</u>

Notes:

Equipment

	£
Original cost of equipment sold	40,000
Accumulated depreciation (3 years @ £8,000)	<u>24,000</u>
Net book value	16,000
Sale proceeds	<u>30,000</u>
Profit on sale (split equally between production and administration)	<u>14,000</u>

Depreciation of premises (1% × 300,000)

= <u>£3,000</u> (split equally between production, administration and distribution)

Depreciation of equipment $(20\% \times 100,000)$

= £20,000 (split equally between production and administration)

Depreciation of vehicles $25\% \times (170,000 - 58,500) = £27,875$ (distribution)

Bright Red Ltd balance sheet as at 31 December 2007

	£ Cost	£ Acc dep	£ Net book value
Fixed assets			
Premises	300,000	26,200	273,800
Equipment	100,000	51,000	49,000
Vehicles	170,000	86,375	83,625
	570,000	163,575	406,425
Current assets			
Stock		44,000	
Debtors (93,600 − 5,200 − 4,420)		83,980	
Prepayments		11,200	
		139,180	
Current liabilities			
Trade creditors	61,560		
Accrued expenses	7,000		
Taxation	19,720		
Debenture interest	6,000		
Proposed dividend	12,000		
Bank overdraft	11,420	117,700	
Net current assets			21,480
			427,905

Long term liability

6% Debentures	<u>100,000</u>
	<u>327,905</u>

Represented by:

Share capital

Ordinary shares	300,000

Reserves

Retained profit	<u>27,905</u>
(19,740 + 8,165)	<u>327,905</u>

Suggested answer: Clear Blue Ltd

Clear Blue Ltd Cash Flow Statement for the year ended 31 December 2007 (indirect method)

	£000	£000
Cash flows from operating activities		
Operating profit		4,144
Adjustments for:		
Depreciation		630
Stock		(1,350)
Debtors		300
Creditors		<u>100</u>
Net cash from operating activities		3,824
Returns on investment and servicing of finance		
Interest paid		(74)
Taxation		(1,000)

Capital expenditure

Purchase of fixed assets	(1,100)	
Receipts from sales of fixed assets	<u>170</u>	(930)

Equity dividends paid	(2,220)
Financing	
Issue of ordinary shares	–
Increase in loan	<u>200</u>
Decrease in cash	(<u>200</u>)

Note

Profit before tax is stated after deducting interest. Therefore operating profit = profit before tax + interest = 4,070 + 74 = 4,144.

T accounts for fixed assets, taxation and dividends

Fixed assets – cost account

		£000			£000
01/01/07	Balance b/f	2,500		Transfer disposals a/c	600
	Additions	<u>1,100</u>	31/12/07	Balance c/f	<u>3,000</u>
		<u>3,600</u>			<u>3,600</u>
01/01/08	Balance b/f	3,000			

Fixed assets – depreciation account

		£000			£000
	Transfer disposals a/c	350	01/01/07	Balance b/f	1,000
			31/12/07	Profit and	
31/12/07	Balance c/f	<u>1,200</u>		loss a/c	<u>550</u>
		<u>1,550</u>			<u>1,550</u>
			01/01/08	Balance b/f	1,200

Fixed assets – disposals account

	£000			£000
Transfer fixed assets' cost a/c	600		Transfer fixed assets depreciation a/c	350
			Cash	80
		31/12/07	Profit and loss a/c (loss on sale)	170
	600			600

Taxation account

		£000			£000
	Cash	1,000	01/01/07	Balance b/f	1,900
			31/12/07	Profit and loss a/c	1,500
31/12/07	Balance c/f	2,400			
		3,400			3,400
			01/01/08	Balance b/f	2,400

Dividends account

		£000			£000
	Cash – interim	720	01/01/07	Balance b/f	1,500
	Cash – final	1,500			
			31/12/07	Profit and loss a/c	2,320
31/12/07	Balance c/f	1,600			
		3,820			3,820
			01/01/08	Balance b/f	1,600

part three*

success in your exams: study, writing and revision skills

General introduction

If you work your way carefully through this part you should at the end be soundly equipped to profit from your lectures, benefit from your seminars, construct your essays efficiently, develop effective revision strategies and respond comprehensively to the pressures of exam situations.

In the six sections that lie ahead you will be presented with:

- checklists and bullet points to focus your attention on key issues;
- exercises to help you participate actively in the learning experience;
- illustrations and analogies to enable you to anchor learning principles in every day events and experiences;
- worked examples to demonstrate the use of such features as structure, headings and continuity;
- tips that provide practical advice in nutshell form.

The overall aim of this part is to point you to the keys for academic and personal development. The twin emphases of academic development and personal qualities are stressed throughout. By giving attention to these factors you will give yourself the toolkit you will need to excel in your studies.

1	
how to get the most out of your lectures	

This section will show you how to:

- make the most of your lecture notes;
- prepare your mind for new terms; and concepts
- develop an independent approach to learning;
- write efficient summary notes from lectures;
- take the initiative in building on your lectures.

Keeping in context

According to higher educational commentators and advisors, best quality learning is facilitated when it is set within an overall learning context. It should be the responsibility of your tutors to provide a context for you to learn in, but it is your responsibility to see the overall context, and you can do this even before your first lecture begins. Such a panoramic view can be achieved by becoming familiar with the outline content of both a given subject and the entire study programme. Before you go into each lecture you should briefly remind yourself of where it fits into the overall scheme of things. Think, for example, of how more confident you feel when you move into a new city (for example, to attend university) once you become familiar with your bearings, that is, where you live in relation to college, shops, stores, buses, trains, places of entertainment, etc.

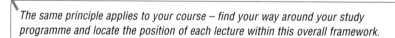

The same principle applies to your course – find your way around your study programme and locate the position of each lecture within this overall framework.

Use of lecture notes

It is always beneficial to do some preliminary reading before you go into a lecture. If lecture notes are provided in advance (for instance, electronically), then print these out, read over them and bring them with you to the lecture. You can insert question marks on issues where you will need further clarification. Some lecturers prefer to provide full notes, some prefer to make skeleton outlines available and some prefer to issue no notes at all! If notes are provided, take full advantage and supplement these with your own notes as you listen. In a later section on memory techniques you see that humans possess ability for 're-learning savings', that is, it is easier to learn material the second time round, as it is evident that we have a capacity to hold residual memory deposits. So some basic preparation will equip you with a great advantage – you will be able to 'tune in' and think more clearly about the lecture than you would have done without the preliminary work.

> *If you set yourself too many tedious tasks at the early stages of your academic programme you may lose some motivation and momentum. A series of short, simple, achievable tasks can give your mind the 'lubrication' you need. For example, you are more likely to maintain preliminary reading for a lecture if you set modest targets.*

Mastering technical terms

Let us assume that in an early lecture you are introduced to a series of new terms such as 'paradigm', 'empirical' and 'zeitgeist'. If you are hearing these and other terms for the first time, you could end up with a headache! New words can be threatening, especially if you have to face a string of them in one lecture. The uncertainty about the new terms may impair your ability to benefit fully from the lecture and therefore hinder the quality of your learning. Subjects such as financial accounting require technical terms and the use of them is unavoidable. However, when you have heard a term a number of times it will not seem as daunting as it initially was. It is claimed that individuals may have particular strengths in the scope of their vocabulary. Some people may have a good recognition vocabulary – they immediately know what a word means when they read it or hear it in context. Others have a good command of language when they speak – they have an ability to recall words freely. Still others are more fluent in recall when they write – words seem to flow rapidly for them when they engage in the dynamics of writing. You can work at developing all three approaches in your course, and the checklist below the next paragraph may be of some help in mastering and marshalling the terms you hear in lectures.

In terms of learning new words, it will be very useful if you can first try to work out what they mean from their context when you first encounter them. You might be much better at this than you imagine especially if there is only one word in the sentence that you do not understand. It would also be very useful if you could obtain a small indexed notebook and use this to build up your own glossary of terms. In this way you could include a definition of a word, an example of its use, where it fits into a theory and any practical application of it.

Checklist for mastering terms used in your lectures:

✓ Read lecture notes before the lectures and list any unfamiliar terms.

✓ Read over the listed terms until you are familiar with their sound.

✓ Try to work out meanings of terms from their context.

✓ Do not suspend learning the meaning of a term indefinitely.

✓ Write out a sentence that includes the new word (do this for each word).

✓ Meet up with other students and test each other with the technical terms.

✓ Jot down new words you hear in lectures and check out the meaning soon afterwards.

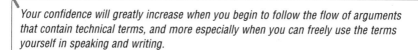

Your confidence will greatly increase when you begin to follow the flow of arguments that contain technical terms, and more especially when you can freely use the terms yourself in speaking and writing.

Developing independent study

In the current educational ethos there are the twin aims of cultivating teamwork/group activities and independent learning. There is not necessarily a conflict between the two, as they should complement each other. For example, if you are committed to independent learning you have more to offer other students when you work in small groups, and you will also be prompted to follow up on the leads given by them. Furthermore, the guidelines given to you in lectures are designed to lead you into deeper independent study. The issues raised in lectures are pointers to provide direction and structure for your extended personal pursuit. Your aim should invariably be to build on what you are given, and you should never think of merely returning the bare bones of the lecture material in a course work essay or exam.

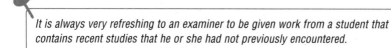

It is always very refreshing to an examiner to be given work from a student that contains recent studies that he or she had not previously encountered.

Note taking strategy

Note taking in lectures is an art that you will only perfect with practice and by trial and error. Each student should find the formula that works best for him or her. What works for one, does not work for the other. Some students can write more quickly than others, some are better at shorthand than others and some are better at deciphering their own scrawl! The problem will always be to try to find a balance between concentrating beneficially on what you hear, with making sufficient notes that will enable you to comprehend later what you have heard. You should not, however, become frustrated by the fact that you will not understand or remember immediately everything you have heard.

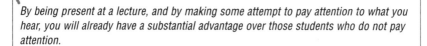

By being present at a lecture, and by making some attempt to pay attention to what you hear, you will already have a substantial advantage over those students who do not pay attention.

Guidelines for note taking in lectures

- Develop the note taking strategy that works best for you.
- Work at finding a balance between listening and writing.
- Make some use of optimal shorthand (for example, a few key words may summarise a story).
- Too much writing may impair the flow of the lecture for you.
- Too much writing may impair the quality of your notes.
- Some limited notes are better than none.
- Good note taking may facilitate deeper processing of information.
- It is essential to 'tidy up' notes as soon as possible after a lecture.
- Reading over notes soon after lectures will consolidate your learning.

Developing the lecture

Some educationalists have criticised the value of lectures because they allege that these are a mode of merely 'passive learning'. This can certainly be an accurate conclusion to arrive at (that is, if students approach lectures in the wrong way) and lecturers can work to devise ways of making lectures more interactive. For example, they can make use of interactive handouts or by posing questions during the lecture and giving time out for students to reflect on these. Other possibilities are short discussions at given junctures in the lecture or use of small groups within the session. As a student you do not have to go into a lecture in passive mode and you can ensure that you are not merely a passive recipient of information by taking steps to develop the lecture yourself. A list of suggestions is presented below to help you take the initiative in developing the lecture content.

Checklist to ensure that the lecture is not merely a passive experience:

- ✓ Try to interact with the lecture material by asking questions.
- ✓ Highlight points that you would like to develop in personal study.
- ✓ Trace connections between the lecture and other parts of your study programme.
- ✓ Bring together notes from the lecture and other sources.
- ✓ Restructure the lecture outline into your own preferred format.
- ✓ Think of ways in which aspects of the lecture material can be applied.
- ✓ Design ways in which aspects of the lecture material can be illustrated.
- ✓ If the lecturer invites questions, make a note of all the questions asked.
- ✓ Follow up on issues of interest that have arisen out of the lecture.

> *You can contribute to this active involvement in a lecture by engaging with the material before, during and after it is delivered.*

2	
how to make the most of seminars	

This section will show you how to:

- be aware of the value of seminars;
- focus on links to learning;
- recognise qualities you can use repeatedly;
- manage potential problems in seminars;
- prepare yourself adequately for seminars.

Not to be underestimated

Seminars are often optional in a degree programme and are sometimes poorly attended because they are underestimated. Some students may be convinced that the lecture is the truly authoritative way to receive quality information. Undoubtedly, lectures play an important role in an academic programme, but seminars have a unique contribution to learning that will complement lectures. Other students may feel that their time would be better spent in personal study. Again, private study is unquestionably essential for personal learning and development, but you will nevertheless diminish your learning experience if you neglect seminars. If seminars were to be removed from academic programmes, then something really important would be lost.

Checklist – some useful features of seminars:

✓ can identify problems that you had not thought of;
✓ can clear up confusing issues;
✓ allow you to ask questions and make comments;
✓ can help you develop friendships and teamwork;
✓ enable you to refresh and consolidate your knowledge;
✓ can help you sharpen motivation and redirect study efforts.

An asset to complement other learning activities

In higher education at the present time there is emphasis on variety – variety in delivery, learning experience, learning styles and assessment methods. The seminar is deemed to hold an important place within the overall scheme of teaching, learning and assessment. In some programmes the seminars are directly linked to the assessment task. Whether or not they have such a place in your course, they will provide you with a unique opportunity to learn and develop.

In a seminar you will hear a variety of contributions, and different perspectives and emphases. You will have the chance to interrupt and to experience being interrupted! You will also learn that you can get things wrong and still survive! It is often the case that when one student admits that they did not know some important piece of information, other students quickly follow on to the same admission in the wake of this. If you can learn to ask questions and not feel stupid, then seminars will give you an asset for learning and a life long educational quality.

Creating the right climate in seminars

In lectures your main role is to listen and take notes, but in seminars there is the challenge to strike the balance between listening and speaking. It is important to make a beginning in speaking even if it is just to repeat something that you agree with. You can also learn to disagree in an agreeable way. For example, you can raise a question against what someone else has said and pose this in a good tone, for example, 'If that is the case, does that not mean that …'. In addition it is perfectly possible to disagree with others by avoiding personal attacks, such as, 'that was a really stupid thing to say', or 'I thought you knew better than that', or 'I'm surprised that you don't know that by now.' Educationalists say that it is important to have the right climate to learn in, and the avoidance of unnecessary conflict will foster such a climate.

Links in learning and transferable skills

An important principle in learning to progress from shallow to deep learning is developing the capacity to make connecting links between themes or topics and across subjects. This also applies to the various learning activities such as lectures, seminars, fieldwork, computer searches and private study. Another factor to think about is, 'What skills can I develop, or improve on, from seminars that I can use across my study programme?' A couple of examples of key skills are the ability to communicate and the capacity to work within a team. These are skills that you will be able to use at various points in your course (transferable skills).

An opportunity to contribute

If you have never made a contribution to a seminar before, you may need something to use as an 'ice breaker'. It does not matter if your first contribution is only a sentence or two – the important thing is to make a start. One way to do this is to make brief notes as others contribute, and whilst doing this, a question or two might arise in your mind. If your first contribution is a question, that is a good start. Or it may be that you will be able to point out some connection between what others have said, or identify conflicting opinions that need to be resolved.

Strategies for benefiting from your seminar experience

If you are required to bring a presentation to your seminar, you might want to consult a full chapter on presentations in a complementary study guide (McIlroy, 2003). Alternatively, you may be content with the summary bullet points presented at the end of this section. In order to benefit from discussions in seminars, some useful summary nutshells are now presented as a checklist.

Checklist – how to benefit from seminars:

- ✓ Do some preparatory reading.
- ✓ Familiarise yourself with the main ideas to be addressed.
- ✓ Make notes during the seminar.
- ✓ Make some verbal contribution, even a question.
- ✓ Remind yourself of the skills you can develop.
- ✓ Trace learning links from the seminar to other subjects/topics on your programme.
- ✓ Make brief bullet points on what you should follow up on.

✓ Read over your notes as soon as possible after the seminar.

✓ Continue discussion with fellow students after the seminar has ended.

If required to give a presentation:

- Have a practice run with friends.
- If using visuals, do not obstruct them.
- Check out beforehand that all equipment works.
- Space out points clearly on visuals (large and legible).
- Time talk by visuals (e.g. 5 slides by 15 minute talk = 3 minutes per slide).
- Make sure your talk synchronises with the slide on view at any given point.
- Project your voice so that all in the room can hear.
- Inflect your voice and do not stand motionless.
- Spread eye contact around audience.
- Avoid twin extremes of fixed gaze at individuals and never looking at anyone.
- Better to fall a little short of time allocation than run over it.
- Be selective in what you choose to present.
- Map out where you are going and summarise main points at the end.

3	
essay writing tips	

This section will show you how to:

- quickly engage with the main arguments;
- channel your passions constructively;
- note your main arguments in an outline;
- find and focus on your central topic questions;
- weave quotations into your essay.

Getting into the flow

In essay writing one of your first aims should be to get your mind active and engaged with your subject. Tennis players like to go out onto the court and hit the ball back and forth just before the competitive match begins. This allows them to judge the bounce of the ball, feel its weight against their racket, get used to the height of the net, the parameters of the court and other factors such as temperature, light, sun and the crowd. In the same way you can 'warm up' for your essay by tossing the ideas to and fro within your head before you begin to write. This will allow you to think within the framework of your topic, and this will be especially important if you are coming to the subject for the first time.

The tributary principle

A tributary is a stream that runs into a main river as it wends its way to the sea. Similarly in an essay you should ensure that every idea you introduce is moving towards the overall theme you are addressing. Your idea might of course be relevant to a subheading that is in turn relevant to a main heading. Every idea you introduce is to be a 'feeder' into the flowing theme. In addition to tributaries, there can also be 'distributaries', which are streams that flow away from the river. In an essay these would represent the ideas that run away from the main stream of thought and leave the reader trying to work out what their relevance may have been. It is one thing to have grasped your subject thoroughly, but quite another to convince your reader that this is the case. Your aim should be to build up ideas sentence-by-sentence and paragraph-by-paragraph, until you have communicated your clear purpose to the reader.

It is important in essay writing that you do not only include material that is relevant, but that you also make the linking statements that show the connection to the reader.

Listing and linking the key concepts

All subjects will have central concepts that can sometimes be usefully labelled by a single word. Course textbooks may include a glossary of terms and these provide a direct route to the beginning of efficient mastery of the topic. The central words or terms are the essential raw materials that you will need to build upon. Ensure that you learn the words and their definitions, and that you can go on to link the key words together so that in your learning activities you will add understanding to your basic memory work.

It is useful to list your key words under general headings if that is possible and logical. You may not always see the connections immediately but when you come back later to a problem that seemed intractable, you will often find that your thinking is much clearer.

EXAMPLE   Write an essay on 'aspects and perceptions of ageing'

You might decide to draft your outline points in the following manner (or you may prefer to use a mind map approach):

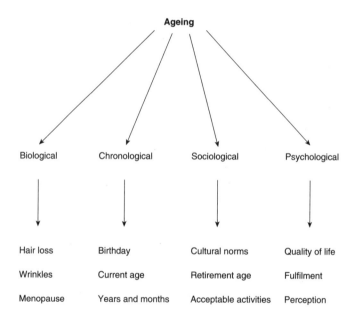

An adversarial system

In higher education students are required to make the transition from descriptive to critical writing. You should think of the critical approach as equivalent to a law case that is being conducted where there is both a prosecution and a defence. Your concern should be for objectivity, transparency and fairness. No matter how passionately you may feel about a given cause you must not allow information to be filtered out because of your personal prejudice. An essay is not to become a crusade for a cause in which the contrary arguments are not addressed in an even handed manner. This means that you should show awareness that opposite views are held and you should at least represent these as accurately as possible.

> *Your role as the writer is like that of the judge in a court of law in that you must ensure that all the evidence is heard, and that nothing will compromise either party.*

Structuring an outline

Whenever you sense a flow of inspiration to write on a given subject, it is essential that you put this into a structure that will allow your inspiration to be communicated clearly. It is a basic principle in all walks of life that structure and order facilitate good communication. Therefore, when you have the flow of inspiration in your essay you must get this into a structure that will allow the examiner to recognise the true quality of your work. For example, you might plan for an introduction, conclusion, three main headings and each of these with several subheadings (see example below). Moreover, you may decide not to include your headings in your final presentation – i.e. just use them initially to structure and balance your arguments. Once you have drafted this outline you can then easily sketch an introduction, and you will have been well prepared for the conclusion when you arrive at that point.

> *A good structure will help you to balance the weight of each of your arguments against each other, and arrange your points in the order that will facilitate the fluent progression of your argument.*

EXAMPLE **Write an essay that assesses the dynamics of the housing market in the decision to purchase or delay**

1 The quest to be on the property ladder:

   a   a house is an investment;

   b   rent payments are a 'black hole' for money;

   c   insufficient quantity of houses for growing needs;

   d   social pressure to be a homeowner.

2 Compounded problems for first time buyers:

    a   delay in purchase to save deposit;

    b   ratio balance of salary against mortgage;

    c   balancing mortgage costs with preferred life-style;

    d   balancing the choice of house with the choice of area.

3 The problem of inflationary pressures:

    a   uncertainty of interest rates and world economies;

    b   income may fall behind inflation;

    c   future house price slumps could create negative equity;

    d   conflicting reports in economic forecasts.

Finding major questions

When you are constructing a draft outline for an essay or project, you should ask what is the major question or questions you wish to address. It would be useful to make a list of all the issues that spring to mind that you might wish to tackle. The ability to design a good question is an art form that should be cultivated, and such questions will allow you to impress your assessor with the quality of your thinking.

> *If you construct your ideas around key questions, this will help you focus your mind and engage effectively with your subject. Your role will be like that of a detective – exploring the evidence and investigating the findings.*

To illustrate the point, consider the example presented below. If you were asked to write an essay about the effectiveness of the police in your local community you might as your starting point pose the following questions.

EXAMPLE   The effectiveness of the police in the local community: initial questions

- Is there a high profile police presence?
- Are there regular 'on the beat' officers and patrol car activities?

- Do recent statistics show increases or decreases in crime in the area?
- Are the police involved in community activities and local schools?
- Does the local community welcome and support the police?
- Do the police have a good reputation for responding to calls?
- Do the police harass people unnecessarily?
- Do minority groups perceive the police as fair?
- Do the police have an effective complaints procedure to deal with grievances against them?
- Do the police solicit and respond to local community concerns?

Rest your case

It should be your aim to give the clear impression that your arguments are not based entirely on hunches, bias, feelings or intuition. In exams and essay questions it is usually assumed (even if not directly specified) that you will appeal to evidence to support your claims. Therefore, when you write your essay you should ensure that it is liberally sprinkled with citations and evidence. By the time the assessor reaches the end of your work, he or she should be convinced that your conclusions are evidence based. A fatal flaw to be avoided is to make claims for which you have provided no authoritative source.

Give the clear impression that what you have asserted is derived from recognised sources (including up-to-date). It also looks impressive if you spread your citations across your essay rather than compressing them into a paragraph or two at the beginning and end.

Some examples of how you might introduce your evidence and sources are provided below:

According to O'Neil (1999) …
Wilson (2003) has concluded that …
Taylor (2004) found that …
It has been claimed by McKibben (2002) that …
Appleby (2001) asserted that …
A review of the evidence by Lawlor (2004) suggests that …

It is sensible to vary the expression used so that you are not monotonous and repetitive, and it also improves variety to introduce researchers' names at various places in the sentence (not always at the beginning). It is advisable to choose the expression that is most appropriate – for example, you can make a stronger statement about reviews that have identified recurrent and predominant trends in findings as opposed to one study that appears to run contrary to all the rest.

> Credit is given for the use of caution and discretion when this is clearly needed.

Careful use of quotations

Although it is desirable to present a good range of cited sources, it is not judicious to present these as 'patchwork quilt' – i.e. you just paste together what others have said with little thought for interpretative comment or coherent structure. It is a good general point to aim to avoid very lengthy quotes – short ones can be very effective. Aim at blending the quotations as naturally as possible into the flow of your sentences. Also it is good to vary your practices – sometimes use short, direct, brief quotes (cite page number as well as author and year), and at times you can summarise the gist of a quote in your own words. In this case you should cite the author's name and year of publication but leave out quotation marks and page number.

> Use your quotes and evidence in a manner that demonstrates that you have thought the issues through, and have integrated them in a manner that shows you have been focused and selective in the use of your sources.

In terms of referencing, practice may vary from one discipline to the next, but some general points that will go a long way in contributing to good practice are:

- If a reference is cited in the text, it must be in the list at the end (and vice-versa).
- Names and dates in text should correspond exactly with list in references or bibliography.
- Lists of references and bibliographies should be in alphabetical order by the surname (not the initials) of the author or first author.
- Any reference you make in the text should be traceable by the reader (they should clearly be able to identify and trace the source).

A clearly defined introduction

In an introduction to an essay you have the opportunity to define the problem or issue that is being addressed and to set it within context. Resist the temptation to elaborate on any issue at the introductory stage. For example, think of a composer of music who throws out hints and suggestions of the motifs that the orchestra will later develop. What he or she does in the introduction is to provide little tasters of what will follow in order to whet the audience's appetite. If you go back to the analogy of the tennis match, you can think of the introduction as marking out the boundaries of the court in which the game is to be played.

If you leave the introduction and definition of your problem until the end of your writing, you will be better placed to map out the directions that will have been taken.

Conclusion – adding the finishing touches

In the conclusion you should aim to tie your essay together in a clear and coherent manner. It is your last chance to leave an overall impression in your reader's mind. Therefore, you will at this stage want to do justice to your efforts and not sell yourself short. This is your opportunity to identify where the strongest evidence points or where the balance of probability lies. The conclusion to an exam question often has to be written hurriedly under the pressure of time, but with an essay (course work) you have time to reflect on, refine and adjust the content to your satisfaction. It should be your goal to make the conclusion a smooth finish that does justice to the range of content in summary and succinct form. Do not underestimate the value of an effective conclusion.

'Sign off' your essay in a manner that brings closure to the treatment of your subject.

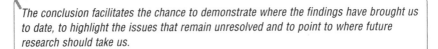

The conclusion facilitates the chance to demonstrate where the findings have brought us to date, to highlight the issues that remain unresolved and to point to where future research should take us.

Top-down and bottom-up clarity

An essay gives you the opportunity to refine each sentence and paragraph on your word processor. Each sentence is like a tributary that leads into the stream of the paragraph that in turn leads into the mainstream of the essay. From a 'top-down' perspective (i.e. starting at the top with your major outline points), clarity is facilitated by the structure you draft in your outline. You can ensure that the subheadings are appropriately placed under the most relevant main heading, and that both sub and main headings are arranged in logical sequence. From a 'bottom-up' perspective (i.e. building up the details that 'flesh out' your main points), you should check that each sentence is a 'feeder' for the predominant concept in a given paragraph. When all this is done you can check that the transition from one point to the next is smooth rather than abrupt.

Checklist – summary for essay writing:

- ✓ Before you start – have a 'warm up' by tossing the issues around in your head.
- ✓ List the major concepts and link them in fluent form.
- ✓ Design a structure (outline) that will facilitate balance, progression, fluency and clarity.
- ✓ Pose questions and address these in critical fashion.
- ✓ Demonstrate that your arguments rest on evidence and spread cited sources across your essay.
- ✓ Provide an introduction that sets the scene and a conclusion that rounds off the arguments.

4	
revision hints and tips	

This section will show you how to:

- map out your accumulated material for revision;
- choose summary tags to guide your revision;
- keep well-organised folders for revision;
- make use of effective memory techniques;
- do revision that combines bullet points and in-depth reading;
- profit from the benefits of revising with others;
- attend to the practical exam details that will help keep panic at bay;
- use strategies that keep you task-focused during the exam;
- select and apply relevant points from your prepared outlines.

The return journey

In a return journey you will usually pass by all the same places that you had already passed when you were outward bound. If you had observed the various landmarks on your outward journey your would be likely to remember them on your return. Similarly, revision is a means to 'revisit' what you have encountered before. Familiarity with your material can help reduce anxiety, inspire confidence and fuel motivation for further learning and good performance.

> *If you are to capitalise on your revision period, then you must have your materials arranged and at hand for the time when you are ready to make your 'return journey' through your notes.*

Start at the beginning

Strategy for revision should be on your mind from your first lecture at the beginning of your academic term. You should be like the squirrel that stores up nuts for the winter. Do not waste any lecture, tutorial, seminar, group discussion, etc., by letting the material evaporate into thin air. Get into the habit of making a few guidelines for revision after each learning activity. Keep a folder, or file, or little notebook that is reserved for revision and write out the major points that you have learnt. By establishing this regular practice you will find that what you have learnt becomes consolidated in your mind, and you will also be in a better position to 'import' and 'export' your material both within and across subjects.

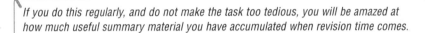

If you do this regularly, and do not make the task too tedious, you will be amazed at how much useful summary material you have accumulated when revision time comes.

Compile summary notes

It would useful and convenient to have a little notebook or cards on which you can write outline summaries that provide you with an overview of your subject at a glance. You could also use treasury tags to hold different batches of cards together whilst still allowing for inserts and re-sorting. Such practical resources can easily be slipped into your pocket or bag and produced when you are on the bus or train or whilst sitting in a traffic jam. They would also be useful if you are standing in a queue or waiting for someone who is not in a rush! A glance over your notes will consolidate your learning and will also activate your mind to think further about your subject. Therefore it would also be useful to make note of the questions that you would like to think about in greater depth. Your primary task is to get into the habit of constructing outline notes that will be useful for revision, and a worked example is provided below.

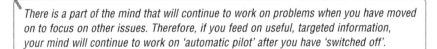

There is a part of the mind that will continue to work on problems when you have moved on to focus on other issues. Therefore, if you feed on useful, targeted information, your mind will continue to work on 'automatic pilot' after you have 'switched off'.

Keep organised records

People who have a fulfilling career have usually developed the twin skills of time and task management. It is worth pausing to remember that you can use your academic training to prepare for your future career in this respect. Therefore, ensure that you do not fall short of your potential because these qualities have not been cultivated. One important tactic is to keep a folder for each subject and divide this topic-by-topic. You can keep your topics in the same order in which they are presented in your course lectures. Bind them together in a ring binder or folder and use subject dividers to keep them apart. Make a numbered list of the contents at the beginning of the folder, and list each topic clearly as it marks a new section in your folder. Another important practice is to place all your notes on a given topic within the appropriate section and don't put off this simple task. Do it straightaway. Notes may come from lectures, seminars, tutorials, Internet searches, personal notes, etc. It is also essential that when you remove these for consultation that you return them to their 'home' immediately after use.

> *Academic success has as much to do with good organisation and planning, as it has to do with ability. The value of the quality material you have accumulated on your academic programme may be diminished because you have not organised it into an easily retrievable form.*

Use past papers

Revision will be very limited if it is confined to memory work. You should by all means read over your revision cards or notebook and keep the picture of the major facts in front of your mind's eye. It is also, however, essential that you become familiar with previous exam papers so that you will have some idea of how the questions are likely to be framed. Therefore, build up a good range of past exam papers (especially recent ones) and add these to your folder. When cows and sheep have grazed, they lie down and 'chew the cud'. That is, they regurgitate what they have eaten, chew it and take time to digest the food thoroughly.

> *If you think over previous exam questions, this will help you not only to recall what you have deposited in your memory, but also to develop your understanding of the issues. The questions from past exam papers, and further questions that you have developed yourself, will allow you to 'chew the cud'.*

Worked example – evaluate the pleasures and problems of keeping a pet

Immediately you can see that you will require two lists and you can begin to work on documenting your reasons under each as below:

Problems

- vet and food bills;
- restrictions on holidays/weekends away;
- friends may not visit;
- allergies;
- smells and cleanliness;
- worries about leaving pet alone.

Pleasures

- companionship;
- fun and relaxation;
- satisfaction from caring;
- cuddles;
- contact with other pet owners;
- good distraction from problems.

You will have also noticed that the word 'evaluate' is in the question – so your mind must go to work on making judgements. You may decide to work through problems first and then through pleasures, or it may be your preference to compare point by point as you go along. Whatever conclusion you come to may be down to personal subjective preference but at least you will have worked through all the issues from both stand-points. The lesson is to ensure that part of your revision should include critical thinking as well as memory work.

You cannot think adequately without the raw materials provided by your memory deposits.

Employ effective mnemonics (memory aids)

The Greek word from which 'mnemonics' is derived refers to a tomb – a structure that is built in memory of a loved one, friend or respected person. 'Mnemonics' can be simply defined as aids to memory – devices that will help you recall information that might otherwise be difficult to retrieve from memory. For example, if you find an old toy in the attic of your house, it may suddenly trigger a flood of childhood memories associated with it. Mnemonics can therefore be thoughts of as keys that open memory's storehouse.

Visualisation is one technique that can be used to aid memory. For example, the Location method is where a familiar journey is visualised and you can 'place' the facts that you wish to remember at various landmarks along the journey – e.g. a bus stop, a car park, a shop, a store, a bend, a police station, traffic lights, etc. This has the advantage of making an association of the information you have to learn with other material that is already firmly embedded and structured in your memory. Therefore, once the relevant memory is activated, a dynamic 'domino effect' will be triggered. However, there is no reason why you cannot use a whole toolkit of mnemonics. Some examples and illustrations of these are presented below.

> *If you can arrange your subject matter in a logical sequence this will ensure that your series of facts will also connect with each other and one will trigger the other in recall.*

Location method – defined above.

Visualisation – turn information into pictures – e.g. the example given about the problems and pleasures of pets could be envisaged as two tug-of-war teams that pull against each other. You could visualise each player as an argument and have the label written on his or her tee shirt. The war could start with two players and then be joined by another two and so on. In addition you could compare each player's weight to the strength of each argument. You might also want to make use of colour – your favourite colour for the winning team and the colour you dislike most for the losers!

Alliteration's artful aid – find a series of words that all begin with the same letter.

Peg system – 'hang' information onto a term so that when you hear the term you will remember the ideas connected with it (an umbrella term). In the example on ageing there were four different types – biological, chronological, sociological and psychological. Under biological you could remember, menopause, hair loss, wrinkling, vision loss, hearing deterioration, etc.

Hierarchical system – this is a development of the previous point with higher order, middle order and lower order terms. For example you could think of the continents of the world (higher order), and then group these into the countries under them (middle order). Under countries you could have cities, rivers and mountains (lower order).

Acronyms – take the first letter of all the key words and make a word from these. An example from business is SWOT – Strengths, Weaknesses, Opportunities and Threats.

Mind maps – these have become very popular. They allow you to draw lines that stretch out from the central idea and to develop the subsidiary ideas in the same way. It is a little like the pegging and hierarchical methods combined and turned sideways! The method has the advantage of giving you the complete picture at a glance, although they can become a complex work of art!

Rhymes and chimes – words that rhyme and words that end with a similar sound (e.g. commemoration, celebration, anticipation). These provide another dimension to memory work by including sound. Memory can be enhanced when information is processed in various modalities – e.g. hearing, seeing, speaking, visualising.

> *You can use memory devices either at the stage of initial learning or when you later return to consolidate.*

Alternate between methods

It is not sufficient to present outline points in response to an exam question (although it is better to do this than nothing if you have run out of time in your exam). Your aim should be to put 'meat on the bones' by adding substance, evidence and arguments to your basic points. You should work at finding the balance between the two methods – outline revision cards might be best reserved for short bus journeys, whereas extended reading might be better employed for longer revision slots at home or in the library. Your ultimate goal should be to bring together an effective, working approach that will enable you to face your exam questions comprehensively and confidently.

> *In revision it is useful to alternate between scanning over your outline points, and reading through your notes, articles, chapters, etc. in an in-depth manner. Also, the use of different times, places and methods will provide you with the variety that might prevent monotony and facilitate freshness.*

Revising with others

If you can find a few other students to revise with, this will provide another fresh approach to the last stages of your learning. First ensure that others carry their work load and are not merely using the hard work of others as a short cut to success. Of course you should think of group sessions as one of the strings on your violin, but not the only string. This collective approach would allow you to assess your strengths and weaknesses (showing you where you are off track), and to benefit from the resources and insights of others. Before you meet up you can each design some questions for the whole group to address. The group could also go through past exam papers and discuss the points that might provide an effective response to each question. It should not be the aim of the group to provide standard and identical answers for each group member to mimic. Group work is currently deemed to be advantageous by educationalists, and team work is held to be a desirable employability quality.

Each individual should aim to use their own style and content whilst drawing on and benefiting from the group's resources.

Checklist – good study habits for revision time:

✓ Set a date for the 'official' beginning of revision and prepare for 'revision mode'.

✓ Do not force cramming by leaving revision too late.

✓ Take breaks from revision to avoid saturation.

✓ Indulge in relaxing activities to give your mind a break from pressure.

✓ Minimise or eliminate use of alcohol during the revision season.

✓ Get into a good rhythm of sleep to allow renewal of your mind.

✓ Avoid excessive caffeine especially at night so that sleep is not disrupted.

✓ Try to adhere to regular eating patterns.

✓ Try to have a brisk walk in fresh air each day (e.g. in the park).

✓ Avoid excessive dependence on junk food and snacks.

5	
tips on interpreting essay and exam questions	

This section will show you how to:

- focus on the issues that are relevant and central;
- read questions carefully and take account of all the words;
- produce a balanced critique in your outline structures;
- screen for the key words that will shape your response;
- focus on different shades of meaning between 'critique', 'evaluate', 'discuss' and 'compare and contrast'.

What do you see?

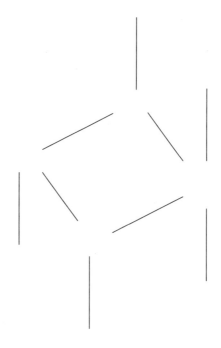

The suggested explanation for visual illusions is the inappropriate use of cues – i.e. we try to interpret three-dimensional figures in the real world with the limitations of a two dimensional screen (the retina in the eye). We use cues such as shade, texture, size, background, etc., to interpret distance, motion, shape, etc., and we sometimes use these inappropriately. Another visual practice we engage in is to 'fill in the blanks' or join up the lines (as in the case of the 9 lines above – we might assume to be a chair). Our tendency is to impose the nearest similar and familiar template on that which we think we see. The same occurs in the social world – when we are introduced to someone of a different race we may (wrongly) assume certain things about them. The same can also apply to the way you read exam or essay questions. In these cases you are required to 'fill in the blanks' but what you fill in may be the wrong interpretation of the question. This is especially likely if you have primed yourself to expect certain questions to appear in an exam, but it can also happen in course work essays. Although examiners do not deliberately design questions to trick you or trip you up, they cannot always prevent you from seeing things that were not designed to be there. When one student was asked what the four seasons are, the response given was, 'salt, pepper, mustard and vinegar'. This was not quite what the examiner had in mind!

> Go into the exam room, or address the course work essay, well prepared, but be flexible enough to structure your learnt material around the slant of the question.

A politician's answer

Politicians are renowned for refusing to answer questions directly or for evading them through raising other questions. A humorous example is that when a politician was asked, 'Is it true that you always answer questions by asking another?', the reply given was, 'Who told you that?' Therefore, make sure that you answer the set question, although there may be other questions that arise out of this for further study that you might want to highlight in your conclusion. As a first principle you must answer the set question and not another question that you had hoped for in the exam or essay.

Do not leave the examiner feeling like the person who interviews a politician and goes away with the impression that the important issues have been sidestepped.

EXAMPLE   Discuss the strategies for improving the sale of fresh fruit and vegetables in the market place at the point of delivery to the customer

Directly relevant points:

- stall and fruit kept clean;
- well presented/arranged produce;
- use of colour and variety;
- position of stall in market (e.g. smells);
- use of free samples;
- appearance and manner of assistants;
- competitive prices.

Less relevant points:

- advantages of organic growth;
- arguments for vegetarianism;
- cheaper transport for produce;
- value of locally grown produce;
- strategies for pest control in growth;
- arguments for refrigeration in transit;
- cheaper rents for markets.

Although some of the points listed in the second column may be relevant to sales overall, they are not as directly relevant to sales 'in the market place at the point of delivery to the customer'. If the question had included the quality of the produce then some of those issues should be addressed. Also it could be argued that some of these issues could be highlighted on a board at the stall, e.g. 'Only organically grown produce is sold at this stall'. So some of the points could be mentioned briefly in this way without going off on a tangent.

Be ready to resist the wealth of fascinating material at your disposal that is not directly relevant to your question.

Missing your question

A student bitterly complained after an exam that the topic he had revised so thoroughly had not been tested in the exam. The first response to that is that students should always cover enough topics to avoid selling themselves short in the exam – the habit of 'question spotting' is always a risky game to play. However, the reality in the anecdotal example was that the question the student was looking for was there, but he had not seen it. He had expected the question to be couched in certain words and he could not find these when he scanned over the questions in blind panic. Therefore, the simple lesson is always read over the questions carefully, slowly and thoughtfully. This practice is time well spent.

You can miss the question if you restrict yourself to looking for a set form of words and if you do not read over all the words carefully.

Write it down

If you write down the question you have chosen to address, and perhaps quietly articulate it with your lips, you are more likely to process fully its true meaning and intent. Think of how easy it is to misunderstand a question that had been put to you verbally because you have misinterpreted the tone or emphasis.

If you read over the question several times you should be aware of all the key words and will begin to sense the connections between the ideas, and will envisage the possible directions you should take in your response.

Take the following humorous example:

(a) What is that on the road ahead?
(b) What is that on the road, a head?

Question (a) calls for the identification of an object (what is that?), but question (b) has converted this into an object that suggests there has been a decapitation! Ensure, therefore, that you understand the direction the question is pointing you towards so that you do not go off at a tangent. One word in the question that is not properly attended to can throw you completely off track as in the following example:

(a) Discuss whether the love of money is the root of all evil.
(b) Discuss whether money is the root of all evil.

These are two completely different questions as (a) suggests that the real problem with money is inherent in faulty human use – that is, money itself may not be a bad thing if it is used as a servant and not a master. Whereas (b) may suggest that behind every evil act that has ever been committed, money is likely to have been implicated somewhere in the motive.

Pursue a critical approach

In degree courses you are usually expected to write critically rather than merely descriptively, although it may be necessary to use some minimal descriptive substance as the raw material for your debate.

EXAMPLE   Evaluate the evidence whether the American astronauts really walked on the moon, or whether this was a stage-managed hoax in a studio

Arguments for studio:

- Flag blowing on moon?
- Explain the shadows.
- Why no stars seen?
- Why little dust blowing at landing?
- Can humans survive passing through the radiation belt?

Arguments for walking:

- Communicates with laser reflectors left on moon.
- Retrieved rocks show patterns that are not earthly.
- How could such a hoax be protected?
- American activities were monitored by Soviets.
- Plausible explanations for arguments against walking.

Given that the question is about a critical evaluation of the evidence, you would need to address the issues one by one from both standpoints.

What you should not do is digress into a tangent about the physical characteristics of the Apollo space ship or the astronauts' suits. Neither should you be drawn into a lengthy description of lunar features and contours even if you have in-depth knowledge of these.

Analyse the parts

In an effective sports team the end product is always greater than the sum of the parts. Similarly, a good essay cannot be constructed without reference to the parts. Furthermore, the parts will arise as you break down the question into the components it suggests to you. Although the breaking down of a question into components is not sufficient for an excellent essay, it is a necessary starting point.

> To achieve a good response to an exam or essay question, aim to integrate all the individual issues presented in a manner that gives shape and direction to your efforts.

EXAMPLE 1   Discuss whether the preservation and restoration of listed buildings is justified

Two parts to this question are clearly suggested – preservation and restoration, and you would need to do justice to each in your answer. Other issues that arise in relation to these are left for you to suggest and discuss. Examples might be finance, prioritisation, poverty, beauty, culture, modernisation, heritage and tourism.

EXAMPLE 2   Evaluate the advantages and disadvantages of giving students course credit for participation in experiments

This is a straightforward question in that you have two major sections – advantages and disadvantages. You are left with the choice of the issues that you wish to address, and you can arrange these in the order you prefer. Your aim should be to ensure that you do not have a lopsided view of this even if you feel quite strongly one way or the other.

EXAMPLE 3   Trace in a critical manner western society's changing attitudes to the corporal punishment of children

In this case you might want to consider the role of governments, the church, schools, parents and the media. However, you will need to have some reference points to the past as you are asked to address the issue of change. There would also be scope to look at where the strongest influences for change arise and where the strongest resistance comes from. You might argue that the changes have been dramatic or evolutionary.

Give yourself plenty of practice at thinking of questions in this kind of way – both with topics on and not on your course. Topics not on your course that really interest you may be a helpful way to 'break you in' to this critical way of thinking.

When asked to discuss

Students often ask how much of their own opinion they should include in an essay. In a discussion, when you raise one issue, another one can arise out of it. One tutor used to introduce his lectures by saying that he was going to 'unpack' the arguments. When you unpack an object (such as a new desk that has to be assembled), you first remove the overall packaging, such as a large box, and then proceed to remove the covers from all the component parts. After that you attempt to assemble all the parts, according to the given design, so that they hold together in the intended manner. In a discussion your aim should not just be to identify and define all the parts that contribute, but also to show where they fit (or don't fit) into the overall picture.

Although the word 'discuss' implies some allowance for your opinion, remember that this should be informed opinion rather than groundless speculation. Also, there must be direction, order, structure and end project.

Checklist – features of a response to a 'discuss' question:

✓ contains a chain of issues that lead into each other in sequence;
✓ clear shape and direction is unfolded in the progression of the argument;
✓ underpinned by reference to findings and certainties;

✓   identification of issues where doubt remains;

✓   tone of argument may be tentative but should not be vague.

If a critique is requested

One example that might help clarify what is involved in a critique is the hotly debated topic of the physical punishment of children. It would be important in the interest of balance and fairness to present all sides and shades of the argument. You would then look at whether there is available evidence to support each argument, and you might introduce issues that have been coloured by prejudice, tradition, religion and legislation. It would be an aim to identify emotional arguments, arguments based on intuition, and to get down to those arguments that really have solid evidence based support. Finally, you would want to flag up where the strongest evidence appears to lie, and you should also identify issues that appear to be inconclusive. It would be expected that you should, if possible, arrive at some certainties.

If asked to compare and contrast

When asked to compare and contrast, you should be thinking in terms of similarities and differences. You should ask what the two issues share in common, and what features of each are distinct. Your preferred strategy for tackling this might be to work first through all the similarities and then through all the contrasts (or vice versa). On the other hand, you might work through a similarity and contrast, followed by another similarity and contrast, etc.

EXAMPLE   Compare and contrast the uses of tea and coffee as beverages

Similarities:

- usually drunk hot;
- can be drunk without food;
- can be taken with a snack or meal;
- can be drunk with milk;
- can be taken with honey, sugar or sweeteners;
- both contain caffeine;
- both can be addictive.

Contrasts:

- differences in taste;
- tea perhaps preferred at night;
- differences in caffeine content;
- coffee more bitter;
- coffee sometimes taken with cream or whiskey;
- each perhaps preferred with different foods;
- coffee preferred for hangover.

> *When you compare and contrast your aim should be to paint a true picture of the full 'landscape'.*

Whenever evaluation is requested

EXAMPLE   TV programme director

Imagine that you are a TV director for a popular television programme. You have observed in recent months that you have lost some viewers to an alternative programme on a rival channel. All is not yet lost because you still have a loyal hard core of viewers who have remained faithful. Your programme has been broadcast for 10 years and there has, until recently, been little change in viewing figures. The rival programme has used some fresh ideas and new actors and has a big novelty appeal. It will take time to see if their level of viewing can be sustained, but you run the risk that you might lose some more viewers at least in the short term.

On the other hand, with some imagination you might be able to attract some viewers back. However, there have been some recent murmurings about aspects of the programme being stale, repetitive and predictable. You have been given the task of evaluating the programme to see if you can ascertain why you have retained the faithful but lost other viewers, and what you could do to improve the programme without compromising the aspects that work. In your task you might want to: review past features (retrospective), outline present features (perspective) and envisage positive future changes (prospective). This illustration may provoke you to think about how you might approach a question that asks you to evaluate some theory or concept in your own academic field of study. Some summary points to guide you are presented below:

- Has the theory/concept stood the test of time?
- Is there a supportive evidence base that would not be easily overturned?
- Are there questionable elements that have been or should be challenged?
- Does more recent evidence point to a need for modification?
- Is the theory/concept robust and likely to be around for the foreseeable future?
- Could it be strengthened through being merged with other theories/concepts?

It should be noted that the words presented in the above examples might not always be the exact words that will appear on your exam paper. For example, you might find 'analyse', or 'outline' or 'investigate', etc. The best advice is to check over your past exam papers and familiarise yourself with the words that are most recurrent.

In summary, this section has been designed to give you reference points to measure where you are at in your studies, and to help you map out the way ahead in manageable increments. It should now be clear that learning should not merely be a mechanical exercise, such as just memorising and reproducing study material. Quality learning also involves making connections between ideas, thinking at a deeper level by attempting to understand your material and developing a critical approach to learning. However, this cannot be achieved without the discipline of preparation for lectures, seminars and exams, or without learning to structure your material (headings and subheadings) and to set each unit of learning within its overall context in your subject and programme. An important device in learning is to develop the ability to ask questions (whether written, spoken or silent). Another useful device in learning is to illustrate your material and use examples that will help make your study fun, memorable and vivid. It is useful to set problems for yourself that will allow you to think through solutions and, therefore, enhance the quality of your learning.

On the one hand there are the necessary disciplined procedures such as preparation before each learning activity and consolidation afterwards. It is also vital to keep your subject materials in organised folders so that you can add/extract/replace materials when you need to. On the other hand there is the need to develop personality qualities such as feeding your confidence, fuelling your motivation and turning stress responses to your advantage. The strategies presented here should help to guide you through finding the balance between these organised and dynamic aspects of academic life.

Your aim should be to become an 'all round student' who engages in and benefits from all the learning activities available to you (lectures, seminars, tutorials, computing, labs, discussions, library work, etc.), and to develop all the academic and personal skills that will put you in the driving seat to academic achievement. It will be motivating and confidence building for you, if you can recognise the value of these qualities, both across your academic programme and beyond graduation to the world of work. They will also serve you well in your continued commitment to life long learning.

6	
exam tips	

This section will show you how to:

- develop strategies for controlling your nervous energy;
- tackle worked examples of time and task management in exams;
- attend to the practical details associated with the exam;
- stay focused on the exam questions;
- link revision outlines to strategy for addressing exam questions.

Handling your nerves

Exam nerves are not unusual and it has been concluded that test anxiety arises because of the perception that your performance is being evaluated, that the consequences are likely to be serious and that you are working under the pressure of a time restriction. However, it has also been asserted that the activation of the autonomic nervous system is adaptive in that it is designed to prompt us to take action in order to avoid danger. If you focus on the task at hand rather than on feeding a downward negative spiral in your thinking patterns, this will help you keep your nerves under control. In the run up to your exams you can practice some simple relaxation techniques that will help you bring stress under control.

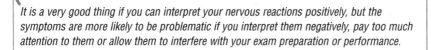

It is a very good thing if you can interpret your nervous reactions positively, but the symptoms are more likely to be problematic if you interpret them negatively, pay too much attention to them or allow them to interfere with your exam preparation or performance.

Practices that may help reduce or buffer the effects of exam stress:

- listening to music;
- going for a brisk walk;
- simple breathing exercises;
- some muscle relaxation;
- watching a film;
- enjoying some laughter;
- doing some exercise;
- relaxing in a bath (with music if preferred).

The best choice is going to be the one (or combination) that works best for you – perhaps to be discovered by trial and error. Some of the above techniques can be practised on the morning of the exam, and even the memory of them can be used just before the exam. For example you could run over a relaxing tune in your head, and have this echo inside you as you enter the exam room. The idea behind all this is, first, stress levels must come down, and second, relaxing thoughts will serve to displace stressful reactions. It has been said that stress is the body's call to take action, but anxiety is a maladaptive response to that call.

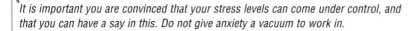

It is important you are convinced that your stress levels can come under control, and that you can have a say in this. Do not give anxiety a vacuum to work in.

Time management with examples

The all-important matter as you approach an exam is to develop the belief that you can take control over the situation. As you work through the list of issues that you need to address, you will be able to tick them off one by one. One of the issues you will need to be clear about before the exam is the length of time you should allocate to each question. Sometimes this can be quite simple (although it is always necessary to read the rubric carefully) – e.g. if two questions are to be answered in a two hour paper, you should allow one hour for each question. If it is a two-hour paper with one essay question and 5 shorter answers, you could allow one hour for the essay and 12 minutes each for the shorter questions. However, you always need to check out the weighting for the marks on each question, and you will also need to deduct whatever time it takes you to read over the paper and to choose your questions. See if you can work out a time management strategy in each of the following scenarios. More importantly, give yourself some practice on the papers you are likely to face.

Remember to check if the structure of your exam paper is the same as in previous years, and do not forget that excessive time on your 'strongest' question may not compensate for very poor answers to other questions. Also ensure that you read the rubric carefully in the exam.

Examples for working out the division of exam labour by time:

1   a 3-hour paper with 4 compulsory questions (equally weighted in marks);
2   a 3-hour paper with 2 essays and 10 short questions (each of the three sections carry one third of the marks);
3   a 2-hour paper with 2 essay questions and 100 multiple-choice questions (two thirds of the marks are on the two essays and one third of the marks are on the multiple choice section).

Get into the calculating frame of mind and be sure to have the calculations done before the exam. Ensure that the structure of the exam has not changed since the last one. Also deduct the time taken to read over the paper in allocating time to each question.

Suggested answers to questions in the box:

1 This allows 45 minutes for each question (4 questions × 45 minutes = 3 hours). However, if you allow 40 minutes for each question this will give you 20 minutes (4 questions × 5 minutes) to read over the paper and plan your outlines.

2 In this example you can spend 1 hour on each of the two major questions, and 1 hour on the 10 short questions. For the two major questions you could allow 10 minutes for reading and planning on each, and 50 minutes for writing. In the 10 short questions, you could allow 6 minutes in total for each (10 questions × 6 minutes = 60 minutes). However, if you allow approximately 1 minute reading and planning time, this will allow 5 minutes' writing time for each question.

3 In this case you have to divide 120 minutes by 3 questions – this allows 40 minutes for each. You could for example allow 5 minutes reading/planning time for each essay and 35 minutes for writing (or 10 minutes reading/planning and 30 minutes writing). After you have completed the two major questions you are left with 40 minutes to tackle the 100 multiple-choice questions.

You may not be able to achieve total precision in planning time for tasks, but you will have a greater feeling of control and confidence if you have some reference points to guide you.

Task management

After you have decided on the questions you wish to address, you then need to plan your answers. Some students prefer to plan all outlines and draft work at the beginning, whilst other prefer to plan and address one answer before proceeding to address the next question. Decide on your strategy before you enter the exam room and stick to your plan. When you have done your draft outline as rough work, you should allocate an appropriate time for each section. This will prevent you from excessive treatment of some aspects whilst falling short on other parts. Such careful planning will help you achieve balance, fluency and symmetry.

Keep awareness of time limitations and this will help you to write succinctly.
Stay focused on the task and don't allow yourself to dress up your responses with
unnecessary padding.

Some students put as much effort into their rough work as they do into their exam essay.

An over elaborate mind map may give the impression that the essay is little more than a
repetition of this detailed structure, and that the quality of the content has suffered
because too much time was spent on the plan.

Attend to practical details

This short section is designed to remind you of the practical details that should be attended to in preparation for an exam. There are always students who turn up late, or go to the wrong venue, or arrive at the wrong exam, or do not turn up at all! Check and re-check that you have all the details of each exam correctly noted. What you don't need is to arrive late and then have to tame your panic reactions. The exam season is the time when you should aim to be at your best.

Arrive at the right venue in good time so that you can quieten your mind and bring your
stress under control.

Make note of the following details and check that you have taken control of each one.

Checklist – practical exam details

✓   Check that you know the correct venue.
✓   Make sure you know how to locate the venue before the exam day.

✓ Ensure that the exam time you have noted is accurate.

✓ Allow sufficient time for your journey and consider the possibility of delays.

✓ Bring an adequate supply of stationery and include back up.

✓ Wear a watch for your time and task management.

✓ You may need some liquid such as a small bottle of still water.

✓ You may also need to bring some tissues.

✓ Observe whatever exam regulations your university/college has set in place.

✓ Fill in required personal details before the exam begins.

7	
be a winner: success in your financial accounting exams	

To succeed in your financial accounting examinations here are ten key points that specially relate to financial accounting that you must always bear in mind.

Hint 1

Success in financial accounting comes at the price of hard and sustained work. There is never any substitute for effort and detailed studying. Financial accounting is best understood by learning the theory and practice of each topic on a week-by-week basis over the course of your studies. It is not a discipline that lends itself to very last minute revision – especially if you wish to obtain the top grades. Prepare a revision timetable allocating a reasonable daily amount of time to your studies. Remember: study regularly and thoroughly during the whole of your course or module.

Understand your syllabus. Study the course/module syllabus in detail. Identify the significant areas. At the commencement of your course of study, you may have been given a short list of what are known as 'learning outcomes'. A learning outcome is a statement of what is expected of a student at the end of a course. For example, a learning outcome might be: 'On completion of this module or course you will be expected to understand the preparation of final accounts.' If you have been supplied with these learning outcomes ensure that you can fully meet them. By understanding the extent of your syllabus and the nature of the learning outcomes, you can help to ensure that you are revising the appropriate topics.

Hint 2

Most financial accounting examinations include both theoretical and practical aspects. Some students may find the practical issues more interesting than the theoretical topics or vice versa. As a result, students who over-concentrate on one aspect of their course or module are immediately placing themselves at a significant disadvantage in their examinations. The only solution is for you to revise both practical and theoretical topics.

Hint 3

Ensure you understand the layout of a trading and profit and loss account, a balance sheet and a simple cash flow statement. In examination questions you will *not* normally be provided with the layout of these statements. You must commit the layout of these statements to memory. Take a blank sheet of paper and keep practising the preparation of the layout until you are confident that you are able to produce this statement every time and without errors. Most financial accounting examinations will have at least one question in some form on these topics – so do not throw away marks – ensure you fully understand this aspect.

Hint 4

Head up your financial statements fully and properly and with the correct date and with the name of the business. Underline the headings – use a ruler – never free hand.

For example:

ABC Ltd
Balance Sheet as at 31 December 2007

Hint 5

Always provide your workings. It is often preferable to prepare your workings on a separate page at the start of your answer.

Head up the page: 'WORKINGS' and underline the word.
Then state what workings you are providing.
For example, if you are calculating the increase in the provision for doubtful debts then head up your workings as:
WORKINGS

Calculation 1:
Increase in provision for doubtful debts.
Then underline your final answer in your workings in the calculation and then move on to:
Calculation 2: ... etc.

It is so easy to make 'silly' errors in the pressurised setting of the examination room and if you provide the wrong answer and fail to give any supporting calculations or workings, you will not obtain marks. So it is always recommended that all workings are provided. At least you may then obtain some marks for your correct workings even if the final answer is wrong.

Hint 6

Look at your course syllabus again. Try to identify the key topics such as stock valuation, depreciation, accruals and prepayments and other accounting adjustments, etc., and ensure that each topic is revised thoroughly.

Then try to obtain past examination papers that have been previously set for students. Examine the layout of the examination paper, the number of questions on the paper, the choice of questions, etc., and then ask yourself a key question:

If I were attempting this examination paper, would I be reasonably confident of passing?

If the answer is no then do something about it – quickly! Revisit your notes, read around the topic again, refer to more than one textbook and then practise former questions again.

Hint 7

Ensure good presentation and layout of your answers.

Whilst a poorly, untidy or sloppily presented answer will not necessarily mean that you will fail – it will certainly not help your case if you are a borderline pass/fail student. Scripts that are well structured, tidily written and well presented can sometimes make the difference between a fail at, say 48 or 49 per cent and a pass grade at 50 per cent.

An impressive exam script can often have a psychological impact on the examiner who may have a few marks to award for well structured layout and presentation. Do not waste even one mark – one day this one mark may make all the difference to you. Ensure your script is tidy, clearly written and always use a ruler to underline.

Hint 8

In the examination itself, time management is vital.

Check how long your examination will last before the day of the examination and then recheck again on the day of your examination by reading the instructions on your examination paper. Then during the examination itself allocate your time to each question. It is a good idea to relate the percentage of marks obtainable from each question to the time available for the whole paper.

For example, if, during a three hour examination, question 1 is for 25 per cent of the marks then do not spend more than 45 minutes (25 per cent of three hours) on this question.

It is essential that once you have spent 45 minutes working on question 1 you must *stop* and move on to the next question – even if you have not completely finished question 1. *Never break this rule.* So remember to check your watch or the examination clock frequently throughout the whole time of the examination.

Hint 9

Sometimes when you have finished a question – such as a set of financial statements – the balance sheet, for example, might not balance. The chances are that you have made an error. It may be a trivial and seemingly insignificant mistake – perhaps a simple addition error – but even so your balance sheet does not now balance. The first point is do not worry. It may be that the error is minor that only perhaps has one half of a mark attached or you may have hit the incorrect key on your calculator. If this is the case then it will have little significant effect on your final mark for the examination paper. It is not worth concerning yourself too deeply and find your performance being affected in later questions. The second point is do *not* spend more than a minute or so searching for your error. It is just not worthwhile. Unless the mistake is blindingly obvious, in the pressure of an examination, the chances are that you will not find the error. It is much better to leave the question and move on to the next question.

Time is too precious to spend looking for mistakes in examinations.

Hint 10

Always check your examination timetable in advance. You must check and check again the time, date and location of your examination. This may sound obvious and indeed it is – but some students invariably misread their examination timetable. Do not fail the examination even before you sit the paper because you have misread the starting time.

In the examination room itself, always read the instructions carefully on the examination paper before you start.

Ensure you check the time allowed for the paper and the number of questions you are required to attempt.

Remember, if you carefully follow these key hints you will considerably improve your chances of passing examinations.

Further reading

McIlroy, D. (2003) *Studying at University: How to be a Successful Student.* London: Sage.

glossary	

Accountability

The responsibility or obligation to provide information and explanations relating to the control and use of business resources.

Accounting equation

A formula whereby a company's total assets must equal its total liabilities plus owners' equity.

Accounting Standards Board (ASB)

The ASB is the standard setting body in the UK that is recognised by section 256 of the Companies Act 1985. The ASB issues *Financial Reporting Standards* and has nine members appointed by the Financial Reporting Council.

Accruals concept

Transactions are accounted for when revenues and expenses are earned or incurred and not necessarily when they are received or paid. Sometimes referred to as 'matching concept'.

Accrued expense

An expense that has been incurred within a financial period but has not yet been paid.

Accrued income

Income that has been earned but not yet received.

Acid test ratio

An accounting ratio that is used in assessing the liquidity of a business. It is defined as (current assets – stock) : current liabilities. Sometimes termed **quick ratio**.

Appropriation account

The part of the profit and loss account which explains how the profit or loss has been allocated to dividends and reserves.

Asset	Any tangible or intangible item to which a value can be assigned. The Accounting Standards Board's *Statement of Principles* defines assets as 'rights or other access to future economic benefits controlled by an entity as a result of past transactions or events'.
Audit	A systematic evaluation of the transactions and financial records of an organisation.
Authorised share capital	The maximum amount of shares that a company can issue to shareholders; this amount is normally stated in the notes to the accounts.
Bad debt	A debt which is uncollectable e.g. because of the financial collapse of the customer (debtor).
Balance sheet	A financial statement identifying the assets, liabilities, and equity of a business at a given point in time.
Bookkeeping	The process of recording the everyday transactions of the activities of a business.
Capital	The funds that are invested in a business.
Capitalisation	To include an item in the balance sheet.
Cash accounting	In cash accounting, only amounts actually received and paid are taken into account.
Cash flow	The amount of cash received by and paid out of a business.
Cash flow statement	A formal accounting statement that identifies movements in cash receipts and payments.
Closing stock	The stock remaining at the close of an accounting period. Closing stock is shown in

both the trading account and the balance sheet.

Companies Acts Legislation in the UK that regulates the activities of companies.

Company An entity that has a legal identity separate from that of its shareholding owners.

Cost of sales The cost of goods that have been sold during the financial year.

Credit The right hand side of an account.

Creditors Amounts owing to a business (e.g. for the provision of unpaid goods and services).

Current assets Items that are not intended for continuing use in a business e.g. stock, debtors and cash. Such assets are normally readily convertible into cash.

Current liabilities Items that fall due for payment within one year of the balance sheet date e.g. creditors.

Current ratio The relationship between current assets and current liabilities, i.e. CA : CL, and is used to assess a company's liquidity.

Debit The left hand side of an account.

Debt (long term) An amount or other liability owed by a business to an external party financing the business. Long term debt is frequently used to refer to the long term borrowings (e.g. a long term loan) of a business.

Debtors Customers who have not yet paid cash.

Depreciation The extent to which an asset has been used up in generating benefits.

Dividends	The return of a proportion of profits to shareholders as a reward for investing in a company.
Doubtful debts	Amounts owing to a business that may not necessarily be collected (e.g. because of the liquidation of a debtor).
Earnings	The net profits of a company after deducting interest and tax but before deducting ordinary dividends.
Efficient markets hypothesis	Share prices instantly adjust to accurately reflect all publicly available information.
Equity	The issued ordinary share capital that, when included with reserves, is classified as shareholders' funds.
Expense	A cost incurred in buying goods or services which is set against a company's revenue to determine profit.
FIFO	First In First Out is a method which assumes that the first stock received is the first stock to be sold to a customer or issued to production.
Final accounts	The financial statements of a business that are prepared at the end of an accounting period. These statements normally include the profit and loss account, the balance sheet and often, a cash flow statement.
Financial accounting	Accounts that are primarily concerned with reporting to external user groups (especially to shareholders).
Financial Reporting Council (FRC)	The UK body established in 1990 that supervises the activities of the Accounting Standards Board.

Financial reporting standards (FRS)	An accounting standard issued by the Accounting Standards Board, first issued in 1991.
Financial statements	Statements which are prepared periodically to provide financial information about the activities of a business; they consist primarily of statements such as the profit and loss account, balance sheet and cash flow statement.
Gearing	Referred to as 'leverage' in the US. The relationship between the funds of a business provided by shareholders and by its other longterm source of funds, often carrying a fixed interest charge (i.e. it is the relationship between debt and equity).
Going concern	The assumption that a business will continue to trade for the foreseeable future.
Goodwill	An intangible asset of a business that includes items such as reputation or expertise for which a purchaser will be expected to pay a premium to acquire. (Another way to express this term is that goodwill is the difference between the price paid for a business and the value of the net tangible assets acquired in return.)
Gross profit	The amount by which sales (revenue) exceeds the cost of sales (cost of goods sold).
Income statement	Also referred to as 'profit and loss account'. A financial statement of a business that identifies revenues, expenses and profits.
Incomplete records	Accounting records that are unfinished or missing and not kept in double entry format.
Intangible asset	A non-monetary asset that is not of a physical or tangible composition, e.g. licences, trade marks and goodwill.

International Accounting Standards (IAS)	Technically, the accounting standards issued by the former IASC. However, the term 'international accounting standards' is often used to refer to both IAS and IFRS.
International Accounting Standards Board (IASB)	The standard setting board of the International Accounting Standards Committee Foundation. The IASB has issued International Financial Reporting Standard (IFRS) since 2001.
International Accounting Standards Committee (IASC)	The predecessor to the IASB. The IASC issued International Accounting Standards (IAS).
International Accounting Standards Committee Foundation	Formed in 2001, it is the parent entity of the IASB.
International financial reporting standards (IFRS)	Accounting standards issued by the International Accounting Standards Board.
Inventory	US equivalent to 'stock' in UK.
Issued share capital	Shares in a company that have actually been taken up by shareholders.
LIFO	Last in first out is a method of stock valuation that assumes the most recently acquired items are the first items to be issued or sold.
Limited liability	The liability of a member (shareholder) of a company that is normally restricted to the amount invested in the company.
Limited liability company	A company that has a separate legal identity from that of its shareholding owners. Normally, the shareholders' liability for the company's debts and obligations are limited to the extent of their investment in the company.

Ltd	Abbreviation which refers to a company with limited liability whose shares are not quoted on a stock exchange.
Liquidity	A condition that refers to the cash resources (or cash equivalents) of a business.
Management accounting	The provision of accounting services to meet specifically the needs of the managers of a business e.g. budgeting and costing.
Margin (gross)	The difference between sales and cost of sales (= gross profit). Margin can also mean gross profit divided by sales.
Mark up	The amount by which sales exceed cost of sales (= gross profit). Mark up can also mean gross profit divided by cost of sales.
Net assets	The total assets (fixed assets plus current assets) of a business minus its total liabilities (long term liabilities plus current liabilities).
Net book value	The value of a fixed asset after deducting accumulated depreciation.
Net capital employed	Net capital employed is defined as total assets (i.e. fixed assets plus current assets) minus current liabilities.
Net profit	Excess of revenue over all expenses. (May be calculated before or after tax.)
Opening stock	The stock of a business at the beginning of an accounting period. Opening stock is shown in the trading account.
Operating profit	Profit after depreciation but before deduction of interest.
Overdraft	The amount (in absolute terms) of a bank current account which has a negative balance.

Paid up shares	The total of the nominal value of the share capital that has been paid by the shareholders.
Partnership	Where two or more individuals agree to trade by sharing risks and profits.
Petty cash	A small amount of cash which is used for minor business expenses.
Plc	Abbreviation which refers to a company with limited liability whose shares can be quoted on a stock exchange.
Prepayments	Expenses which have been paid for in advance of receiving benefits at the balance sheet date.
Price earnings ratio	A company's market share price divided by its earnings per share.
Profit	The excess of revenue over expenses.
Profit and loss account	Also referred to as 'income statement'. A financial statement of a business that identifies revenues, expenses and profits.
Proprietorship	The interest of the owner in a business.
Provision for doubtful debts	An accounting estimate of the proportion of debts that may eventually need to be written off.
Quick ratio	See 'acid test ratio'.
Realised profits	Profits that have been objectively verified by the evidence of a sale.
Reliability	Where accounting information is free from material error or bias.
Relevance	To be relevant, information must normally be capable of influencing an economic decision of a user.

Reserves	Profits and capital gains made by a company in previous accounting periods that have not been distributed to shareholders.
Retained profits	Profits that have not been distributed to shareholders as dividends but instead have been reinvested in the company.
Return on capital employed (ROCE)	Profit expressed as a percentage of the resources which a business has at its disposal. Normally, the profit before interest and tax is compared to net assets, or profit before interest and tax is compared to net capital employed.
Return on equity	Profit (normally profit after tax) expressed as a percentage of shareholders' funds.
Revaluation (of assets)	Increase or decrease in a company's assets to take account of inflation or changes in the value of assets since they were acquired.
Rights issue	Method of raising capital that gives existing shareholders the right to subscribe to additional shares.
Share capital	Part of the owners' equity and equal to the number of a company's issued shares at their nominal value.
Share premium	Amount payable for a share above its nominal price.
Shareholder	A member of a company limited by shares.
Shareholders' funds	Share capital plus reserves.
Statements of Standard Accounting Practice (SSAP)	These were accounting standards issued by the former Accounting Standards Committee (ASC). The first SSAP was issued in 1971 and the ASC was superseded by the Accounting

Standards Board (ASB) in 1990. SSAPs are no longer issued but many have been adopted or sometimes re-issued as Financial Reporting Standards (FRS) by the ASB.

Sole trader   An individual who operates an unincorporated business without partners.

Stewardship   Where the assets of a business are entrusted to another party. For example, shareholders own a company's assets but the company's directors have day-to-day control of these assets. The assets are deemed to be held in stewardship on behalf of the shareholders.

Stock   Referred to as inventories in the US. General term for goods or other assets purchased for resale or purchased for incorporation into the manufacturing of products for later sale.

Stock turnover   A measure of the frequency with which a business, on average, replaces its stock. It is usually defined as the cost of sales divided by average or closing stock.

'T' account   An account that shows debit entries on the left hand side and credit entries on the right hand side.

Tangible assets   Assets that are physical in nature, e.g. land and buildings, plant and machinery.

Tax   A charge levied by government. For example, corporation tax is a specific tax on a company's profit.

Trial balance   A statement listing and totalling both the debit and credit balances from each ledger account.

True and fair view   This term is an overriding legal requirement for the presentation of financial statements of

	UK companies (and also required by the European Union's Fourth Directive).
Unappropriated profits	Profits that have not been withdrawn from a business or used for any other purpose.
Undistributed reserves	Profits and capital gains from current and previous financial years that have not been paid out to shareholders as dividends.
Unrealised profit	A profit or loss that has not been converted into cash or other readily realisable assets (often termed a 'paper' profit or loss).
User groups	Interested parties who may wish to extract information from the financial statements of a company e.g. shareholders, financial institutions, government, etc.
Weighted average cost method (for stocks)	A method of determining the cost of sales and closing stock valuation. This method values stock on the basis of average stock purchases weighted by volume.
Working capital	The difference between the current assets and current liabilities of a business.

references

Atrill, P. and McLaney, E. (2006) *Accounting and Finance for Non-Specialists,* 5th edition, Harlow: Pearson.

Britton, A. and Waterston, C. (2006) *Financial Accounting,* 4th edition, Harlow: Pearson.

Hand, L., Isaaks, C. and Sanderson, P. (2005) *Introduction to Accounting for Non-Specialists,* London: Thomson.

Jones, M. (2006) *Financial Accounting,* Chichester: Wiley.

index

Page numbers in **bold** show an entry in the glossary

balance sheet *cont.*
  provision for doubtful debts,
    38, 42, 62
    example question, 43–4
    worked example, 77–9, 80–1
balance sheet identity, 16
'bank' vs. 'cash', 18
banks
  limitations of financial
    statements, 10
  use of financial statements, 9–10
bookkeeping, 153 *see also* double entry
  bookkeeping
business types, 8–9

capital, 153
  growth potential, 9
  maintaining base through provision
    for depreciation, 46
  withdrawal *see* drawings
capital introduced by owner (CI)
  accounting equation, 19
  recording transactions, 20–1
capitalisation, 153 *see also* market
  capitalisation
carriage inwards, 67
carriage outwards, 67
'cash' vs. 'bank', 18
cash accounting, 153
cash cycle, 83
cash flow, 6, 153
cash flow statement, 4, 69–77, 153
  approach, 70–1
  background, 69
  direct method, 71–2
  example questions, 75–6,
    99–100, 104–5
  indirect method, 72–3
  layout, 148
  rationale, 69–70
Cash Flow Statements (FRS 1), 7, 69
Cash Flow Statements (IAS 7), 69
cash forecasts, 71
claims, 16 *see also* equity; liabilities
closing stock, 67–8, 153–4
  see also stock valuation
Companies Acts, 6, 154
company, 5, 154 *see also* limited
  liability companies; Ltd;
  multinational companies; Plc

company law, 6
comparability, 13
consistency concept, 12
cost of sales (goods sold), 20, 154
  effect of increase in stock, 73
  effect of stock valuation, 30, 34–5
credit, 9, 154
creditors, 154
  and cash flow statements, 74–5
    example, 75–6
  use of financial statements, 9
creditors' payment ratio, 87–8
current assets (CA), 154
  accounting equation, 19
    example question, 21–2, 23
  recording transactions, 20–1
  balance sheet, 60
  prepayments, 27, 29, 63
current (short term) liabilities, 154
  accounting equation, 19
  recording transactions, 20–1
  balance sheet, 61
  accruals, 26, 29, 63
  final dividends, 63
current (working capital) ratio,
    84–5, 154
  company comparison example,
    94, 95
customers
  use of financial statements, 10

debit, 154
debt (long term), 154
  equity: debt ratio *see* gearing
debtors ('accounts receivable'), 19, 154
  and cash flow statements, 74
    example question, 75–6
  terminology, 8
  see also bad debts; doubtful debts
debtors' collection (turnover) ratio, 87
  company comparison example,
    94, 96
Deloitte, 14
depreciation, 45–7, 62, 68, 154
  accounting entries, 51–3
  accounting policy vs. estimation
    technique, 11
  and cash flow statements, 73
    example question, 75–6
  company policy, 51